Georgia

MORE THAN 300 THINGS TO DO
FOR SOUTHERN LOVERS

PATRICK ALLEN

d

HILL STREET PRESS   ATHENS, GEORGIA

A HILL STREET PRESS BOOK

Hill Street Press is committed to preserving the written word. Every effort is made to print books on acid-free paper with a significant amount of post-consumer recycled content.

Text and cover design by Anne Richmond Boston.

Printed in Canada.

Published in the United States of America by:

Hill Street Press LLC
191 East Broad Street, Suite 209
Athens, Georgia 30601-2848 USA
706-613-7200
info@hillstreetpress.com
www.hillstreetpress.com

Front cover postcard:
(Genuine Curteich Chicago) Originally printed by Dixie News Company

Back cover postcard:
(C.T. American Art) Originally published by Lamas Brothers News Company

First edition

2   4   6   8   10   9   7   5   3   1

Library of Congress Catalog Card #98-94100

Contents

INTRODUCTION

ARTS FOR THE HEART   1

Opera   3

Ballet and Dance   5

Music, Music, Music   5

Film   9

Museums   12

Theater (and Dinner Theater)   15

Festivals   17

Spotlight—Romantic Theaters   22

THE GREAT OUTDOORS   25

Covered Bridges   27

Nature   31

Drives   33

Foliage Hikes   34

Gardens   36

Tours   44

Theme Parks   45

Picnic Spots   46

Pick Your Own   47

Festivals   51

Spotlight—Stargazing   54

PLAY ON   57

Up, Up, and Away   60
Love on the Links   61
Love All   63
Saddled For Love   64
Bicycling Tours Made for Two   66
Hiking   68
Snow Skiing   69
Got a Brand-New Pair of Roller Skates   70

MAGIC MOUNTAINS   71

Waterfalls   73
Tubing and Rafting   77
Mountain Inns   78
Golf   84
Spotlight: Mittie's Wedding   85

LOVE ON THE GOLDEN ISLES   87

Savannah   89
The Barrier Islands   95
Tybee Island   95
Ossabaw Island   96
Blackbeard Island   96
Sapelo Island   97
Sea Island   98
Little St. Simons Island   99
St. Simons Island   100
Jekyll Island   102
Cumberland Island   104
Spotlight: Build Your Dream House in a Day   107
Spotlight: The Sweetheart of Mankind   109

WINING, DINING, AND DANCING 111

Table for Two 113

Cooking Schools 118

Wineries 119

Bars 121

Jazz Clubs 122

Dives 123

Dancing 124

OOH LA LA! 129

Indulgence in Atlanta 131

Spas 132

Bed and Breakfast Inns 134

THE UNEXPECTED 137

For Those Who Seek the Unique 139

Poetry with Soul 139

Go Play in the Dirt 140

Glow-in-the-Dark Action 140

Looking for Peace and Quiet 141

Headed to Paradise 141

Go Climb a Tree 142

Be a Kid Again 142

Paradise by the Dashboard Light 143

Give the Outdoors as a Gift 143

Vintage Love 143

Tell the World You're in Love 144

Look to the Heavens 144

INDEX 145

If you would be loved, love and be lovable.—*Benjamin Franklin*

Introduction When I began compiling *Romantic Georgia* I felt I easily had a book's worth of romantic ideas in my own experience. But when I raised the question "What's the most romantic spot in Georgia?" to colleagues and friends at the water cooler or at the dinner table, I quickly learned that others had notions about what is romantic that are as firmly held as they are different from my own. Romance, like beauty, is in the eye of the beholder, and that's the best part about it.

So that's why this book—full of my own ideas and added to by the experience of my card-carrying romantic friends—is as varied as the state itself. The most important thing to remember is that romance is everywhere. While I hope the suggestions in this book are as inspiring as they are diverse, you can find romance as easily in the comfort of your own home as you can on an exotic trip halfway around the world.

I've presented for you and your special someone romantic inspirations for romantic days and nights from the most traditional to the downright offbeat. The variety in what sets peoples' hearts racing come from varying sensibilities, interest, and age. I have tried to include something for everyone, suggestions for almost every corner of the state, for every time of year, for residents and visitors, and for every budget. Whether riding llamas in northeast Georgia followed by a picnic beside a mountain stream or presenting your special someone with a bauble in Tiffany's unmistakable blue box over high tea at Atlanta's Ritz-Carlton Hotel is your idea of romance, I've tried to accommodate your interests and budget. I've organized the ideas around some obvious themes, yet there is a good deal of overlap between the sections and some of the suggestions mentioned in for specific place are as easily found in one area as another. For example, taking a ride on a rented tandem bike is as romantic in Atlanta's Piedmont Park as it is along the state's beaches.

In that way, although I list specific locations and directions in some cases, I hope that you will also use *Romantic Georgia* as an idea book to discover new and exciting things to do throughout the state, as well as in your own backyard.

WHAT IS ROMANTIC, ANYWAY?

The best answer to this question is that there is no one answer to the question. The correct response varies with the couple, how long they've been together, their level of activity, and their interests. Moreover, the question can be answered umpteen different ways in the course of a single weekend. Why not plan a day hike and a night at the ballet for Saturday, and a horseback ride and museum-going for Sunday? You know it will be fun getaway if your luggage is packed with both a tuxedo and bowling shoes.

HOW DO YOU USE THIS BOOK?

Romantic Georgia is organized thematically, so that suggestions for nature lovers can be found in one chapter, for sports fans in another, for culture vultures in another, and so on. If you're trying to plan an outing in a particular city or locate a specific site, your best bet is to use the index. Some of the special sites in Georgia are hard to classify, so I've woven some "Spotlights" between chapters. Furthermore, I wanted to point out some especially important sites in each chapter, so those are set off in sidebars.

To assist those who live in or who are planning to travel to a particular region, I use geographic codes which accompany each entry. These are

 =The Golden Isles and Coastal Georgia

 =The Mountains of Northeast Georgia

 =The Heartland of Georgia: Big Cities and Antebellum Towns

Because the heartland is the largest section geographically and encompasses most of the state's large urban areas, you'll find more entries from that region than from the others.

Each entry includes address and telephone information and a website address when available. In some cases—such as with state parks and lakes—addresses do not appear for obvious reasons. I have also left out the address of some entities when it might prove confusing. The Atlanta Symphony, although obviously based in that city, performs all over the state; your best bet is to call the box office or visit the website for a complete listing. In a few instances, particularly discussing gallery or shopping districts such as Savannah's Founder's Walk, no phone number is given.

ROMANTIC GEORGIA HALL OF FAME

If your romantic engine is so revved you can't take the time to look through the whole book, let me point out what I consider the ten most romantic sites and activities in the state.

- ♥ Enjoy IMAX movies and martinis at Atlanta's Fernbank Museum of Natural History.
- ♥ Sing along at the Blind Willie Blues Festival in Thomson.
- ♥ The Love Affair Fine Arts Festival, with its variety of theatre and music events in the neon-lit Art Deco Tift Theatre, lives up to its inspiring name.
- ♥ A day-trek through the old-growth Chattahoochee National Forest is a romantic must—make the trip on a llama for added fun.
- ♥ Frolic among thousands of butterflys at the enclosed Day Butterfly Gardens at Callaway Gardens.
- ♥ Improve your swing with golf lessons by day, and refine your palate wine tasting by night at The Cloister on Sea Island.
- ♥ Take a biking or hiking tour of the state's covered bridges or waterfalls.
- ♥ Have your romantic message posted on the Jumbotron at Turner Field during an Atlanta Brave's game.

HAVE I LEFT OUT YOUR FAVORITE ROMANTIC THING TO DO IN GEORGIA?

As I mentioned earlier, this book is intended to be an idea book, not an encyclopedic reference. In the appendix, you'll find a list of resources to help you research your own outing, including organizations, publications, and websites.

If you'd like the publisher to consider adding your favorite romantic destinations to a future edition, please write:

Romantic Georgia
c/o Hill Street Press
191 East Broad Street, Suite 209
Athens, GA 30601-2848
info@hillstreetpress.com

Arts
for the
Heart

Life is the flower for which love is the honey.—Victor Hugo

Enjoying the arts together is a perfect way to spend an evening. Whether it is being swept away on the operatic high tide of Verdi's Aida, enjoying a symphony concert and dinner al fresco, or yukking it up at a silent film, the lively arts are essential to romance.

OPERA

Opera must be the most romantic of all the arts. Lush costumes and Latin passion, intrigue and revenge—a Verdi opera might have more gore spilled in the name of love than a week's worth of *Jerry Springer*.

The Atlanta Opera is one of America's premier opera companies. For those unfamiliar with opera, English supertitles are projected on a screen suspended over the stage so everyone can follow along. Its performances of the classic Romantic operas are held in the Fox Theatre.

Atlanta Opera
Suite 620, 1800 Peachtree Street, NW / Atlanta
800-35-OPERA / www.atlantaopera.org

The Fox Theatre
660 Peachtree Street / Atlanta / 404-817-8700
www.thefoxtheatre.com

It is appropriate that Augusta, birthplace of one of America's finest sopranos, Jessye Norman, should have a wonderful company, the Augusta Opera. They perform in the Bell Auditorium or the Imperial Theatre.

Augusta Opera Association
P.O. Box 3865 / Hill Station / Augusta / 706-826-4710

Opera Athens is a small but energetic company which performs classical and contemporary opera. The performances are held in the downtown Morton Theater, a restored 1910 African American vaudeville theater, the only remaining black-built vaudeville theater in America. Duke Ellington, Cab Calloway, Louis Armstrong, Bessie Smith, and other legendary figures once performed there.

Opera Athens
P.O. Box 49194 / Athens / 30601

Morton Theater
195 West Washington Street / Athens / 706-613-3771

The perfect compliment to opera? Italian food, of course. The Capitol City Opera Company in Atlanta performs everything from Puccini to Broadway show tunes in its series of "Short Opera Galas" at the San Gennaro Italian Ristorante. Beautiful music and four-course Italian feasts are served up to opera fans and opera-phobes alike. All meals are prixe fixe, including wine. Receptions with complimentary appetizers precede the performances. Opera highlights and an operalogue are given to each opera-goer. Performances are held the third Tuesday of every month.

San Gennaro Italian Ristorante
2196 Cheshire Bridge Road, NE / Atlanta / 404-633-2848

BALLET AND DANCE

The home theater of the Atlanta Ballet is the Fox Theatre. "The Fabulous Fox," as locals call it, is Atlanta's last great movie palace—an over-the-top, Moorish-style theater built in 1929. It features the constellations of the night sky projected onto its cobalt blue domed ceiling.

Atlanta Ballet
1400 West Peachtree Street, NW / Atlanta / 404-874-7905
www.atlantaballet.com

The Fox Theatre
660 Peachtree Street / Atlanta / 404-881-2100
www.thefoxtheatre.com

The classically trained, culturally diverse Ballethnic Dance Company performs a lively repertoire of jazz- and African American-influenced classical ballet to its enthusiastic audiences. The company was formed by two former dancers with Dance Theater of Harlem.

Ballethnic Dance Company
P.O. Box 7749 / Atlanta / 404-762-6319

MUSIC, MUSIC, MUSIC

The music—such passion and emotion. The audience—so elegant in evening clothes. Whether as a first date or a fiftieth anniversary, a classical concert is something special to share. Georgia boasts many fine symphonies and venues with a romantic mood. The Atlanta Symphony, for instance, hosts a series of "Champagne and Coffee Concerts," and Spivey Hall on the campus of Clayton State University hosts concerts on its magnificent 4,413-pipe Albert Schweitzer Memorial Organ.

♫ **Atlanta Symphony Orchestra**
1280 Peachtree Street, NE / Atlanta / 404-733-5000
www.atlantasymphony.org

♫ **Spivey Hall (on the Clayton State University campus)**
Morrow / 770-961-3683 / www.spiveyhall.org

Perhaps the only way to improve on an evening spent at a concert is to enjoy it outdoors under the twinkling stars. Concerts at Chastain Park Amphitheater are always some of Atlanta's most sought-after tickets. Big name performers in musical genres ranging from classical to alternative perform in the Michelob Light/Coca-Cola Series at one of America's premier outdoor venues. For "table set-up" shows, bring a picnic basket—anything from Baccarat to Tupperware would not be out of place—or pre-order dinner and wine from the theater's in-house caterers (Affairs to Remember, 404-872-7859; or Proof of the Pudding, 404-892-2359; tablecloths and candles are available at an extra charge). Complete meals, gourmet pizzas, specialty sandwiches, and desserts can also be ordered on site from the Chastain Bistro, Starbucks Coffee, and long-time local favorite, Harry's in a Hurry. Individual tickets can be purchased at all TicketMaster locations or charged by phone. Noisy audiences are a perennial problem at Chastain, so be forewarned: while silent snuggling is encouraged, cellular phones, pagers, and whispering are not.

♫ **Chastain Park Amphitheater**
Atlanta / 404-636-5004

♫ **Ticketmaster**
404-249-6400

As beloved by Atlanta lovers as the Atlanta Symphony Orchestra's Chastain concerts are the ASO's regular concerts at Piedmont Park and Centennial Olympic Park. The world famous ASO performs programs of serious and popular music to enthusiastic audiences every year, always graciously for free. The preferred locale is your choice: Piedmont Park is a gently rolling turn-of-the-century park in midtown by the designer of New York's Central Park, Frank Law Olmstead; whereas Centennial Park is a decidedly urban setting among the glittering skyscrapers of Atlanta's downtown. Picnic baskets are recommended in Piedmont Park as there are few take-away restaurants within easy walking distance. Don't forget to pack your sparklers for the annual Independence Day concert.

Atlanta Symphony Orchestra
1280 Peachtree Street, NE / Atlanta / 404-733-5000
www.atlantasymphony.org

The Rome Symphony Orchestra gives two mood-setting performances annually. The "Love in the Evening" concert with the Rome Symphony Chorale in the Rome City Auditorium is a popular event each June. Be sure to pack dancing shoes in your picnic hamper when you go to the Clock Tower Jazz Ensemble's annual concert held the second Saturday in September in Ridge Ferry Park.

Rome Symphony Orchestra
P.O. Box 533 / Rome / 30612-0533 / 706-291-7967
www.romegeorgia.com

The annual June Jazz Candlelight Series takes place every Sunday in June at the Eighth Street Bulkhead on the enchanting Augusta Riverwalk. The site is a natural amphitheater, with the audience overlooking the starlit river and the levee behind holding in the music of the beloved local jazz group, All That Jazz. Picnic baskets and blankets are encouraged. Tradition holds that all concertgoers bring candles to give the concert a romantic glow. The sight of hundreds of flickering candles along the riverfront is unforgettable.

Riverwalk Special Events
Augusta / 706-821-1754

You won't believe the romantic songsters who have come from Georgia: Johnny Mercer, Otis Redding, Lena Horne, and Ray Charles are just a few. The Georgia Music Hall of Fame in downtown Macon is the un-stuffiest museum you're ever likely to visit. Its 43,000 square feet house a non-stop music festival of displays, videos, and light shows thematically organized as the Jazz & Swing Club, Rhythm & Blues, the Skillet Licker Café (country music), and Vintage Vinyl (a rock and roll record store). It's alternately rockin' and romantic.

Georgia Music Hall of Fame
200 Martin Luther King Jr. Boulevard / Macon / 912-750-8555
www.gamusichall.com

Spending the day in the library may not be your idea of romance, but if it's studying up on the life of native Georgian, acclaimed lyricist Johnny Mercer, you may change your tune. Mercer was born in Savannah and in his stellar career penned many of our most-loved mid-century songs of the heart including "Moon River." The Special Collections department at the Pullen Library of Georgia State University houses a Johnny Mercer Museum collection of original scores for his award-winning songs, his letters, photographs, and other materials.

Johnny Mercer Museum
Georgia State University/Pullen Library / Decatur Street
Atlanta / 404-651-2186

Enjoy a mid-week romance break with a Blue Sky Concert on the Square in downtown Decatur every Wednesday in May and

September. The concerts, mostly jazz, take place under the shady canopy of the large oaks of Decatur's historic courthouse. There are a variety of take-away restaurants in the charming shopping district that surrounds the courthouse. The town square has such a small-town, long-ago feel it's hard to believe that it's just a few miles from the hustle and bustle of downtown Atlanta. The weekly concerts are repeated at 7:00 P.M. every Wednesday—again from the Community Bandstand—on the town square for those whose schedules don't permit a little romance during the workday.

City of Decatur
Office of Downtown Development / 404-371-8386

FILM

Wasn't everyone's first date dinner and a movie? But before video rental or generic megaplexes, going to the movies was an event— an occasion to dress up and enjoy the hushed opulence of a movie palace, a world nearly as glamourous as the black-and-white one depicted on the screen.

Sure, eating pizza from a box spread on the coffee table and watching *When Harry Met Sally* on the little screen is romantic, but no comparison to holding hands in the plush velvet seats of Atlanta's 1929 Fox Theatre while watching the best of classic movies. The theater's Summer Film Festival shows everything from *Breakfast at Tiffany's* to *Lawrence of Arabia* to *The Horse Whisperer* in the opulence of the Moorish-style theater. Special treats include a sing-along accompanied by the theater's original Wurlitzer pipe organ. The lyrics of Tin Pan Alley classics flash on the screen so everyone can join in. Just follow the bouncing ball! In addition to soft drinks, the concession stand sells wine, beer, and mixed drinks. The theater is located in midtown Atlanta within easy walking dis-

Made in Georgia
A Trio of
Home-Grown Films

*The state has become a real center
of movie-making in recent years.
Some films made partially or
wholly in Georgia include* Forces
of Nature, Forest Gump,
Midnight in the Garden of
Good and Evil, Drop Squad,
Love Potion #9, The Big Chill,
and The Night the Lights Went
Out in Georgia. *A few of my
favorites, you ask:*

Driving Miss Daisy

*Winner of the Academy Award for
Best Picture in 1989, this drama
traces the twenty-five-year friend-
ship of an Atlanta widow (Jessica
Tandy) and her loyal driver
(Morgan Freeman). The film
adaptation of the eponymous play
by Atlanta playwright Alfred
Uhry used several locations in
Atlanta's Druid Hill and Little
Five Points neighborhoods.*

➢

tance of several romantic restaurants,
including the French bakery Alon's,
directly across the street in the Georgian
Terrace and the retro-diner Mick's, a few
blocks south at the corner of Peachtree
and Pine Streets.

The Fox Theatre
660 Peachtree Street / Atlanta
404-881-2100

Alon's
659 Peachtree Street / Atlanta
404-724-0444

Mick's
557 Peachtree Street / Atlanta
404-688-6425

The Silent Film Society of Atlanta screens
the kind of movies your grandparents
swooned over. The silver screen classics
are shown at the R.R. Theater.

Silent Film Society of Atlanta
Atlanta / 404-633-5131
www.geckoent.com/sfsa/index.html

R.R. Theater
Piedmont Hospital (Building 77)
1968 Peachtree Road / Atlanta

A Laurel and Hardy movie marathon is
the highlight of the Oliver Hardy Festival
held each year in the actor's hometown
of Harlem in Columbia County on the

first Saturday in October. The annual shenanigans include an Oliver Hardy look-alike contest, tricycle races, carnival rides, and a street dance. The festival is held at various sites around Harlem, located on the left soon after exit 61 of I-20 (Harlem/Appling exit). (F.Y.I.—Oliver is the one with the mustache.)

Oliver Hardy Festival
P.O. Box 99 / Harlem / 706-556-3448

City of Harlem
706-556-3448

Can a science museum be a romantic spot? If you've seen the scene in *Annie Hall* in which a rain-soaked Woody Allen and Diane Keaton duck into New York's Museum of Natural History to confess their love, you'll know the answer is a decided "yes." Atlanta's Fernbank Museum of Natural History sponsors wildly popular Friday-night viewings of its nature and adventure films shown in the IMAX Theater, a five-story screen with 12,000 watts of digital sound. Moviegoers can journey inside a volcano or roar across the frozen surface of the North Pole in a helicopter, without spilling a drop of their generously-sized, well-mixed martinis. It's a roller-coaster ride for sophisticates, and some of the action on the immense screen gets so hairy your partner's unconscious grasp of your hand is almost a sure thing. The weekly event begins with live music and cocktails. Be

Cold Sassy Tree

This May-December romance in the turn-of-the-century South starring Faye Dunaway and Richard Widmark was based on Olive Ann Burns's novel of the same name. Scenes from this touching drama were shot in Dahlonega.

Fried Green Tomatoes

Partially filmed in Juliette, Georgia, this adaptation of Fannie Flagg's Fried Green Tomatoes at the Whistle Stop Café *is a funny and move tale of the friendship of three women played by Kathy Bates, Jessica Tandy, and Mary Stuart Masterson.*

sure to visit the Museum's Star Gallery, with its fiber-optic ceiling accurately depicting the stars in the Georgia sky. Tickets can be charged by telephone and sometimes sell out a week in advance.

Fernbank Museum of Natural History
767 Clifton Road / Decatur / 404-370-1822 (Martinis & IMAX hotline)

Its hard for any die-hard romantic to imagine why drive-in movie theaters are fast becoming a thing of the past. But rest assured that this '20s holdover is alive and well at Atlanta's Starlite Six Drive-in Theatre. For only a few dollars, you can chose a double feature of first-run movies viewed from the theatre's six screens (three in winter). Bring your own food and drink, even lawn chairs if you want to spread out. But there's been an improvement since Sandra Dee and Fabian were on the outdoor screen—the sound is provided through your own car radio. Cool daddy-o!

Starlite Six Drive-in Theater
2000 Moreland Avenue, SE / Atlanta / 404-267-5786

MUSEUMS

Museums are so quiet and peaceful they encourage thoughtful strolls. View the Morris Museum of Art's collection of Southern antebellum portraiture or the marvels of ancient Egypt at the Michael C. Carlos Museum and your thoughts will surely turn to romance. (Lunch becomes a romantic interlude in the intimate confines of the beautiful Michael Graves-designed Caffe Antico on the MCCM's top floor.)

Morris Museum of Art
1 Tenth Street / Augusta / 706-724-7501

Carlos Museum of Art
571 Kilgo Circle (on the Emory University campus)
Atlanta / 404-727-4282 / www.emory.edu

The Ships of the Sea Maritime Museum is a perfect place for a romantic afternoon. Located not far from Franklin Square in Savannah, the museum is located in the Scarbrough House, built in 1819 for the principal owner of the Savannah, the first steamship to cross the Atlantic Ocean. The museum has a fine collection of maritime paintings, antiques, and ship models, including one of the 1912 Titanic in mid-sink. The museum boasts the largest garden in the historic district and is listed on the National Register of Historic Places.

The Ships of the Sea Maritime Museum
41 King Boulevard / Savannah / 912-232-1511

Puppets are for kids, right? And, kids at heart. . . . Atlanta boasts one of the best puppetry museums (and theaters) in the country of interest to kids and adults alike. You'll be wowed at the craftsmanship and artistry of their historic collection spanning centuries.

Center for Puppetry Arts
1404 Spring Street / Atlanta / 404-873-3391

The official art museum of the state of Georgia is a treasure on the University of Georgia campus and is unknown to many Georgians. The recently built museum boasts a fine permanent collection and rotating exhibits, including an outstanding print collection and Italian sculpture. There is a café on-site if you're in the mood for a quick sandwich. Otherwise, start or finish your day with a candlelight meal at one of Athens's more romantic restuarants, DePalma's Italian Café or the Last Resort Grill, both in charming downtown Athens. While you're in Athens also make time to stroll around downtown with its abundant funky shops and coffeehouses as well as the eighteenth- and nineteenth-century north quad of the University.

Romantic Bookstores

One of the most romantic things you can do together is visit a local bookstore. Spend an evening browsing the stacks separately and then discuss favorite new and old classics you have (re)discovered. Many bookstores these days have a café within the store or next door where you can spend some time together reading. Most stores' schedules are busy with readings by local authors and nationally recognized writers passing through town. Some stores have book discussion groups that welcome new writers. Many also have wonderful programs for children. A few favorites include:

**E Shaver Fine Books (the owner Esther Shaver is mentioned in the pages of Midnight in the Garden of Good and Evil)
326 Bull Street
Savannah
912-234-7257**

**Final Touch Books
133 E Courthouse Square
Decatur
404-378-5300**

➤

**Georgia Museum of Art
East Campus Drive (next to the new Performing Arts Center)
Athens / 706-542-4462
www.uga.edu/gamuseum/Info.html**

**DePalma's Italian Café
401 East Broad Street / Athens
706-354-6966**

**The Last Resort Grill
184 West Clayton Street / Athens
706-549-0810**

Stargazing is always a romantic thing to do, even in the middle of the afternoon. The Jim Cherry Memorial Planetarium at the Fernbank Science Center is a planeterium theater with a seventy-foot diameter dome onto which 200 separate projectors show the sun; moon; visible planets; 8,900 stars; the Milky Way; and certain nebulae and star clusters. These heavenly bodies traverse the imaginary sky at an accelerated rate, compacting a whole night's worth of skywatching into an hour or two. Some special effects equipment demonstrates phenomena from black holes to rotating galaxies to the rings of Saturn.

**Fernbank Science Center
156 Heaton Park Drive / Atlanta
404-378-4314 x831**

Theater
(and dinner theater)

An evening of dinner and theater is perhaps one of the most popular ways to craft a romantic evening. And good theater abounds in Georgia, from the mainstage to the blackbox, popular productions to new premieres of experimental and small company productions. An evening at the theater is often an architectural treat as well ranging from traditional theater structures with proscenium thrust stages to black boxes ingeniously tucked away into renovated school buildings and converted warehouses. Much of the action is centered in Atlanta but there are noteworthy theater companies across the state. Most theaters are usually surrounded by an excellent choice of restaurants and, if you're not of a mind to make advance plans (and reservations), leave ample time for strolling to find one that suits your needs. A couple of reliable, favorite theater companies in Atlanta to look for include: the Horizon Theater (offering Southeastern and national premieres of contemporary drama), the award-winning Seven Stages Theater (always a sure bet), and Actor's Express Theater. Horizon and Seven Stages are both

Wordsworth Books
2112 N Decatur Road
Decatur
404-633-4275

Charis Books
1189 Euclid Avenue
Atlanta
404-524-0304

OutWrite
991 Piedmont Avenue
Atlanta
404-607-0082

Regina's
4515 Habersham Street
Savannah
912-353-7048

Jackson Street Books (one of the state's best kept secrets; used and rare books)
260 N. Jackson Street
Athens
706-546-0245

also many local, regional, and national chain bookstores across the state such as Barnes & Noble, Books-a-Million, Borders, Chapter 11, B. Dalton, Doubleday, Scribners, and Walden Books. They offer a very broad selection of titles and the larger stores have cafés and author events.

located in the colorful Little Five Points neighborhood in Atlanta which offers plenty of restaurants for dining before of after the performance.

Atlanta's most established house is the Alliance Theater, housed at the Woodruff Performing Arts Center. In Athens, the Town and Gown Players have entertained loyal audiences from across north Georgia for decades with popular favorites.

Seven Stages Theater
1105 Euclid Avenue / Atlanta / 404-523-7647

Horizon Theater
1083 Austin Avenue / Atlanta / 404-584-7450

Actor's Express Theater
887 West Marietta Street / Atlanta / 404-607-7469

Town & Gown Players
Grady Avenue at the Taylor Grady House / Athens
706-548-3854

Alliance Theater
1280 Peachtree Street / Atlanta / 404-733-5000

Agatha's—A Taste of Mystery dinner theater was started by husband-and-wife team John Diehl and Nancy Louis who sought to make the campy audience-participation murder comedies they present as satisfying as their impressive food and wine menu. The audience is encouraged to participate by reading small parts and providing simple sound effects, but true to the company's laid-back approach, no one is ever forced to cut up if they are feeling shy. Performances and the five-course, prix-fixe dinner make a wonderful and wacky three-and-a-half hours.

Agatha's—A Taste of Mystery
693 Peachtree Street, NE / Atlanta / 404-875-1610

The Atlanta Shakespeare Tavern is a place out of time. As in Shakespeare's own day there is live music, hand-sewn costumes, and thrilling sword fights—all as a backdrop to the Bard's tales of passion and tragedy. The theater is paneled in rough-hewn boards and filled with rustic plank dining tables. The British pub menu, notably the potato leek soup and Cornish pastry, is fit for both king and groundling.

Atlanta Shakespeare Tavern
499 Peachtree Street, NE / Atlanta / 404-897-3404

FESTIVALS

The Georgia Renaissance Festival is a fun and campy send-up of a sixteenth-century English country fair. Jousting, grog drinking, and jumbo turkey legs are fit for Henry VIII. The festival is held twice yearly—spring and fall—eight miles south of Atlanta's Hartsfield Airport.

Georgia Renaissance Festival
Atlanta / 770-964-8575 / www.surfrite.com

To salute legendary blues artist Blind Willie, the bluesman's hometown of Thomson holds the Blind Willie Blues Festival every October. Blind Willie McTell knew a thing or two about love and sang and played on his twelve-string guitar standards such as "Broke Down Engine Blues," "Statesboro Blues," and "Love Changing Blues." Hope you have better luck in love than poor Willie did. The festival features blues artists from across the country on sixty-acre site on Stagecoach Road in Thomson, in McDuffie County. (Ironic for a bluesman, McTell is buried in Happy Valley, McDuffie County.)

Thomson-McDuffie Tourism Bureau
111 Railroad Street / Thomson / 706-595-5584
www.thomson.net

The Georgia Shakespeare Festival brings all the passion of the Bard into the present day. Every summer and fall, with periodic holiday performances, the festival celebrates the lives and loves of seventeenth-century England at the Conant Performing Arts Center on the campus of Oglethorpe University. The design of the newly built Center mimics the shape of the Festival's longtime home, a circular tent, and Shakespeare's own Globe Theatre. The auditorium wall can be raised in pleasant weather. Casual clothing, a raucously funny and ribald pre-show on the lawn, picnicking, and first-rate productions make this a perfect venue for romance. A Harris Teeter grocery store in the nearby Brookhaven neighborhood can provide catered picnic dinners to festival-goers. A limited number of pre-made dinners are on hand, but it is preferable to order from Harris Teeter in advance (404.814.5983).

Conant Performing Arts Center
4484 Peachtree Road / Atlanta / Georgia Shakespeare Festival
404-264-0020 / www.gashakespeare.org

The Love Affair Fine Arts Festival, held the first weekend of every May in Tifton, is a celebration of the fine and performing arts. Five stages are in constant use for a variety of theatre and musical events, as is the neon-lit Art Deco Tift Theatre. The annual festival, which also features crafts and international pavilions, is so well done that it was one of the few such events to be named a Cultural Olympiad Event during the 1996 Olympic Games.

Arts Experiment Station
Tifton / 912-386-3558 / blackmar@c.abac.peachnet.edu

Located in shady Rolater Park, just off the Cave Spring town square, the Cave Spring Art Festival is home to a juried art show and fine crafts for sale. Combine the festival's many activities with a tour of the hamlet's namesake limestone cave—home of the Devil's Stool stalagmite formation—and the town's incredible collection of National Register of Historic Places buildings—ninety structures in a town of less than 1,000 residents—and you have a full and romantic day trip. Bring along some empty jugs to sample the renowned water of the Cave Spring. Cave Spring is also home to the Georgia School for the Deaf and many if not most of the local residents and merchants use sign language throughout the course of the day. If you are staying overnight consider the Hearn Academy Inn which is located in a convented school building and offers gracious accomodations.

Cave Spring Arts Festival
Cave Spring / 706-291-7663

Hearn Academy Inn
15 Cedartown Road / Cave Spring / 706-777-8865

Savannah, called the "Hostess City of the South" is, not surprisingly, home to three of the most romantic festivals in Georgia: Wormsloe Celebrates the Founding of Georgia, the Savannah College of Art and Design Sidewalk Arts Festival, and the Tom Turpin Ragtime Festival. At the Wormsloe celebration, one can stroll the mile-and-a-half avenue of live oaks from the weathered gates of the estate to the impressive ruins of the circa-1739 fortified home of Noble Jones, one of Georgia's first colonists. Each step will take you back to the romantic first days of the last English colony. The festival includes costumed reenactors explaining the daily life of this tumultuous period. The SCAD Sidewalk Arts Festival centers around hundreds of works of art created with colored chalk on the sidewalks of the beautiful historic district surrounding the art school—appropriate for the city named the number one walking city in America by *Walking Magazine*. Anyone can join in—just sign up for a box of chalk and a section of sidewalk to create a masterpiece on the sidewalk of Forsyth Park. How about a portrait of your someone special? The festival has live music, campus tours, food, and novelty attractions. Tom Turpin, born in Savannah, was a major force in the development of ragtime music. Events celebrating Turpin and jazz are held throughout the city in late October or early November annually. Wonderfully themed concerts pack the calender: "Ragtime on the Riverboat," "Pianos in the Parlors," and "Ragtime Champagne Breakfast," to name a few. Ragtime dance lessons are given in preparation for the Ragtime Ball. Other events include a Sunday by the Seaside picnic and trolley rides throughout historic Savannah.

Savannah College of Art and Design
Savannah / 912-238-2487

Wormsloe Historic Site
Savannah / 912-353-3023

Tom Turpin Ragtime Society
207 E. 44th Street / Savannah / 912-233-9989

Mossy Creek Barnyard Arts and Crafts Festival, located three miles from Perry, celebrates the rich folk-pottery and craft tradition of northeast Georgia. The best known and most sought-after of these crafts are the face jugs of the Meaders family. The humorously grotesque faces, some with real animal or human teeth, are covered in the woodash- or lime-based alkaline glazes common to the region. The festival features many other mountain crafts, such as angora spinning and soap making, as well as live entertainment. The festival is held every October.

Mossy Creek Barnyard Arts & Crafts Festival
Perry / 912-922-8265

Madison is one of the most popular antebellum towns in Georgia and is conducive to hours if not days of romantic strolling and sightseeing. The main street is lined with one of the best collections of nineteenth century homes in Georgia, most lovingly restored and immaculately maintained. The pride of the town is the Madison-Morgan Cultural Center, a stellar arts center in a restored school building including an intimate theater. There are activities throughout the year, but a real highlight is when the Atlanta Symphony travels to Madison to perform, and tickets go quickly. The town also hosts several organized home tours throughout the year, but the Christmas tour of the town's grandest homes is perhaps the most widely known. Several antique shops pepper the town square accompanied by several restaurants, from home cooking higher-end establishments.

The Madison-Morgan Cultural Center
434 South Main Street / Madison / 706-342-4743

spotlight

ROMANTIC THEATERS

The Fabulous Fox Theatre, one of the oldest operating theaters in the city, nearly fell to the wrecking ball in a development-crazed Atlanta. Saved by a city-wide outcry, it draws huge numbers to its packed schedule of plays, concerts, and film festivals. The crowds are probably at the Fox as much to see the 1929 theater itself as they are to enjoy the on-stage entertainment. Special features include a domed ceiling onto which a pretend sky of emerald blue and twinkling stars is projected before each performance, and a Wurlitzer organ which rises out of the orchestra pit—musician and all—to play period music upon occasion.

The Egyptian Ballroom adjoining the theater is a favorite place for wedding receptions, formal dances, and the like. Restaurants and a piano bar are located on the first floor of the building, fronting world-famous Peachtree Street. Whatever sort of performance you enjoy here, the opulent surroundings of the Fox are sure to give it a romantic mood. Make a special weekend out of your theatre-going by staying at the lovely Georgia Terrace Hotel, a historic landmark located directly across from the theatre. If your visit to the city doesn't allow you to catch an evening performance or weekend matinee, consider taking the Atlanta Preservation Center's enlightening and fact-filled walking tours of the old movie palace.

The Fox Theatre
660 Peachtree Street / Atlanta / 404-881-2100

The Georgian Terrace
659 Peachtree Street / Atlanta / 404-897-1991

Atlanta Preservation Center
Atlanta / 404-876-2041

Built in 1917 after the devastating Augusta fire of the previous year, the Imperial Theater hosted vaudeville in its early days, as well as the original

spotlight

ROMANTIC THEATERS

silent movies and the first "talkies" of the area. Today the stage is the home of the Augusta Opera and the Augusta Ballet, as well as other live events.

Imperial Theatre
745 Broad Street / Augusta / 706-722-8293

The official State Theater of Georgia, the historic Springer Opera House, has has been fully restored to its 1871 glamor and operates as a working theater for performances of every kind. Oscar Wilde once performed there during his U.S. tour.

Springer Opera House
1017 Second Avenue / Columbus / 706-327-3688

The
Great
Outdoors

The Eskimos have fifty-two words for snow because it is so special to them; there ought to be as many for love.—Margaret Atwood

Nothing puts a couple in mind of love more than a day spent in nature. Reflecting on the eternity of a sunset, enjoying a foliage hike, strolling in a garden can all remind you of the central fact of romance: love is the greatest natural wonder.

COVERED BRIDGES

The romance of *The Bridges of Madison County* doesn't entirely explain the appeal covered bridges have for lovers. They seem to act as time tunnels, transporting us back to when everything, including love, was slower and surer. All of the bridges below have picnic spots, and one is your special bridge. The reason bridges were originally covered is more pragmatic than romantic—weatherproof coverings made supporting timbers last three or four times longer than those exposed to the elements. Most covered bridges today are closed to vehicular traffic and some, due to their advanced age, to foot traffic as well, but all have easy nearby access and are bicyclists' and photographers' dreams.

> **The Covered Bridge Trail of Georgia**
> **800-776-7974 / Georgia Department of Transportation**
> **www.dot.state.ga.us/homeoffs/bridge_dsgn.www/covered/index.htm**

The Auchumpkee Creek Bridge was destroyed in 1994, soon after the hundredth anniversary of its construction. It was painstakingly rebuilt using traditional building techniques, including the use of wooden pegs and teams of mules and oxen, thus ensuring its enjoyment by future generations of lovers. The bridge crosses Allen Road off U.S. 80 in Upson County. Consider scheduling your trip to coincide with the Georgia Covered Bridge Arts Festival, which takes place annually in October. In addition to self-guided tours of the bridges and vicinity, there is a juried art show and market on the Thomaston-Upson County Courthouse Square, a benefit tour of homes, and entertainment.

Georgia Covered Bridge Arts Festival
Thomaston / 800-776-7974

Coheelee Creek Bridge is the southernmost historic covered bridge in the United States. Stop by Michelle's restaurant before heading to the wooded picnic site. The bridge crosses Old River Road off Hilton Road in Early County. The Westville historic village and Kolomoki Mounds State Historic Park are nearby. Westville is an outdoor museum of buildings and gardens of the nineteenth century. Several buildings, including a farmhouse, a church, a carriage house, and townhouse—all buildings from the vicinity of Lumpkin in danger of being torn down—were saved from the wrecking ball and moved to the fifty-eight acre campus to be reassembled as a town of the 1850s. Historic crafts and cooking methods are recreated. The Kolomoki Mounds Historic Site in Blakely is the site of a fascinating museum which interprets the history and burial practices of the Native American residents of the area through the seven temple, burial, and ceremonial mounds of the Swift Creek and Weeden Island peoples built in the twelfth and thirteenth centuries.

Michelle's
109 Main Street / Lumpkin / 912-838-9991

🌲 **Westville Village**
Troutman Road off GA Route 27 / Lumpkin / 912-838-6310
www.westville.org

🌲 **Kolomoki Mounds State Historic Park**
Route 1, Box 114 / Blakely / 912-723-5296

The Euharlee Creek Bridge is also known as Lowry Bridge after miller Daniel Lowry who operated the mill a few yards to the northeast. The bridge, constructed in 1866 by master bridge builder and former slave Horace King (1807–1880), is Georgia's oldest covered bridge. Although there are no picnic tables in the area, there are plenty of delightful, grassy fields surrounding "The Timber Tunnel."

🏚 **Euharlee Creek Bridge**
Bartow County (forty-five minutes northwest of Atlanta),
adjacent to County Road 30

The Watson Mill Bridge in George L. Smith Park is sometimes known as Parrish Mill because it has the distinction, unique among Georgia covered bridges, of being attached to and a part of a functioning mill. Parrish Mill is constructed over a power-generating dam across Fifteen Mile Creek. Doors at either end of the mill allow traffic to pass—thus, technically, its also a bridge!

🏚 **George L. Smith State Park**
on SR 23 between Twin City and Metter in Emanuel County

The Stone Mountain Covered Bridge has an interesting history. Constructed in 1891 in Clarke County to span the Oconee River, the bridge was known to generations of University of Georgia students as the College Avenue Bridge. Others knew it as Effie's Bridge, so named because it provided the most direct route from the University of Georgia campus to an Athens bordello operated by a certain Miss Effie. The bridge was moved to Stone Mountain

Park in DeKalb County in 1965 to preserve it. Today, the covered bridge provides access across Stone Mountain Park Lake to the Indian Island picnic area and to the many other attractions of this well-traveled park: a riverboat, a skylift to the top of the granite mountain, a railroad, a museum, and a zoo.

Located just outside the west gate of the park is Stone Mountain Village, a collection of craft shops, vintage and antique furniture galleries, and a variety of restaurants all housed in restored nineteenth century railway buildings. Father's Day weekend, the time of the annual Stone Mountain Village Arts and Crafts Show, is a favorite time for visitors. Stop by the Village's visitor center, housed in a renovated 1915 standard gauge wooded caboose.

Stone Mountain State Park
Highway 78 / Stone Mountain / 800-317-2006

Stone Mountain Village
adjacent to Stone Mountain State Park / 770-879-4971

You probably won't recognize the Stovall Mill Bridge in White County as a location in the 1951 Susan Heyward movie *I'd Climb the Highest Mountain,* but you'll recognize it on first sight as a place for great romance. Located in an area rich in Cherokee history, the Stovall Mill Bridge replaced an earlier bridge washed away in the 1890s. The bridge spans Chickamauga Creek, not to be confused with the larger, better-known creek of the same name located to the north. It is Georgia's narrowest bridge at eleven feet wide—barely wide enough to accommodate a wagon loaded with hay bales.

Stovall Mill Bridge
adjacent to State Road 255 in White County

The Watson Mill Bridge crosses a small fall of the Broad River and a rock shoal, making it the ideal place for a lover's stroll. The

Watson Mill Bridge State Park also contains a charming mill complex, as well as fishing, picnic areas, cabins, and hiking trails. A visit is well recommended.

Watson Mill Bridge
at the border of Oglethorpe and Madison counties

NATURE

Every romance marches along at its own pace in its own direction. To suit every stride, below are suggestions for several different kinds of nature experience: nature walks and tours; fall foliage walks; short hikes of easy to moderate difficulty; and daytrips to tour gardens, botanical gardens, and plantations.

What's romantic about a swamp? Well, you'd be surprised. The Okefenokee Swamp, at over 700 square miles, is one of the most spectacular sites in Georgia (extending into northern Florida). Guided one- and two-hour boat tours of the Okefenokee National Wildlife Refuge are ideal for bird watchers and photographers. If you'd prefer to be alone, boats are available for rental. Arrangements can also be made for overnight tours and camping within the park. On the second Saturday in October annually, locals (and many visitors) celebrate with the Okefenokee Festival. One of the highlights is the "Tour de Swamp" bike race. There are several structures to visit within the swamp, but make sure not to miss the Chesser Family Homestead.

Okefenokee National Wildlife Refuge
Route 2, Box 338 / Folkston / 912-496-3331

The Augusta Canal is an incredibly diverse site for biking, boat rental touring, or walking. All along its meandering course, historic mills and nineteenth-century rowhouses and churches are visible. Interspersed are gorgeous natural features such as a granite quarry basin, lakes, and a fish ladder. It's hard to believe that much of this exists within the civilized confines of Georgia's Garden City. Excellent maps to this remarkable greenspace are available from the Canal Authority. Adjacent to the canal is the beautiful Savannah Rapids Park which offers a stunning view of the rapids as well as excellent bicycling along a scenic 8.5-mile trail leading to downtown Augusta. There are several bicycle rental shops in town: two downtown outlets include Jordan's Bicycle Center and Clyde Dunaway Bicycles.

Augusta Canal Authority
P.O. Box 2367 / Augusta / 706-823-0440

Jordan's Bicycle Center
527 Thirteenth Street / Augusta / 706-724-6777

Clyde Dunaway Bicycles
215 Twelfth Street / Augusta / 706-722-4208

Enjoying fall foliage is a popular experience for all lovers in north Georgia. If your idea of romance is snuggling in the front seat with the lovey-dovey music of native Georgians Ray Charles and Otis Redding playing on the CD, driving tours are provided below. However, if seeing the blush of crisp fall air on your lover's cheeks sets you off, some suggestions for foliage hikes are also provided below. The U.S. Forest Service operates a Leaf Watch hotline to inform us of peak color conditions. In the spring the same areas are resplendent in Brown-Eyed Susans and Yellow Lady Slippers, and you'll hear the sweet songs of the yellow-breasted chat and the "tea-kettle, tea-kettle" of the Carolina wren.

Leaf Watch Hotline
800-532-2521

DRIVES

Travel along the Richard B. Russell Scenic Highway (Georgia Highway 348) near Helen is rewarded with a wonderful show as the road crosses over the Blue Ridge. The road borders the Raven Cliffs Wilderness Area with access to Duke's Creek Falls and the Appalachian Trail.

Scenic Georgia Highway 197 provides an impressive display of autumn color as it twists along beside the Soquee River and Lake Burton in the northeast Georgia mountains. After the famous roller coaster-like dip in the road, a waterfall flows under the road, so closely in fact, you might feel the spray on a windy day.

A four-wheel drive vehicle is not essential, but recommended, for leaf watching on the Patterson Gap Loop. Traveling west on U.S. Highway 76 at Clayton, drive north along Persimmon Road. The real show begins when Persimmon becomes the gravel Patterson Gap Road. After Moon Valley Resort and Betty's Creek, turn right onto Betty Creek Road. Consider stopping at the Dillard House in the town of Dillard, a family-style restaurant famous across the South. Dillard House can have some pretty imposing lines, but the meal is well worth the wait.

While in the area look for the Hambidge Center for the Arts off of Betty Creek Road several miles west of Dillard. This mountain-side outpost is one of the few artist colonies in the state, founded by Mary Hambidge in 1934 to foster local artists, especially weavers. Today, writers, painters, photographers, potters, weavers, and other artists work in residence. The drive through the valley is one of the most scenic and peaceful in the state. The Hambidge Center does not have tours or accommodations for visitors, but stop in briefly when you're in the area.

Dillard House
U.S. 441 / Dillard / 706-746-5348

In the mid-1960s an Athenian named Eliot Wiggington started the nationally known Foxfire Project at the Rabun Gap-Nacoochee School to preserve and continue the study of Appalachian culture and history. *The Foxfire Book* grew into a series of books which are popular nationally to this day. The Foxfire Collections on U.S. Highway 441 in Mountain City is a museum and gift shop dedicated to Foxfire.

🌲 **Foxfire Collections**
U.S. Highway 441 / Mountain City
706-746-5828

One of the most spectacular (and popular) drives in north Georgia is along Georgia Highway 19/129 from Dahlonega to Brasstown Bald. The route winds through stunning mountain scenery, passing by the home of the late poet Byron Herbert Reece and a popular outpost of the Appalachian Trail. Make sure to stop at the Walasi-Yi Center at the crown of the mountain, the border of Union and Lumpkin Counties. It is a perfect example of the stone and timber construction projects of the New Deal-era Civilian Conservation Corps. Today it houses a provisions store for campers as well as a charming gift shop and bookstore with a wonderful selection of books about the Appalachians, pottery and crafts by local mountain artists, and other giftables. Make sure to pick up a volume of poetry by Byron Herbert Reece to read from to your honey as you hike or picnic near the lodge building.

FOLIAGE HIKES
(FROM LEAST TO MOST STRENUOUS)

Fort Mountain State Park in Murray County is Georgia's second-largest state park. The name derives from an ancient rock wall of piled stones which snakes along 885 feet of the dense forest. Its purpose, possibly fortification, is unknown. There are four easy-to-hike trails though the Cohutta Mountains. The 0.5-mile Big Rock Nature Trail has a stream which is neither mapped or named on the U.S. Geological Survey—thus there's no reason you and your partner can't claim it as your own. The 0.7-mile Goldmine Branch Trail crosses the foliage-lined stream four times. The 1.8 miles of inter-connected, color-coded trails, known as the Old Fort Trails have observation decks from which to observe the fall splendor. All the trails in Fort Mountain State Park are clearly mapped and labeled with explanatory signs at the park's entrance.

Cloudland Canyon State Park in Dade County has two impressive options for enjoying fall foliage. The 0.3-mile Waterfall Trail has wooden walkways leading down to the canyon and the sandstone and shale waterfalls of Daniel Creek. The park straddles a deep gorge hewn into Lookout Mountain by Sitton Gulch Creek with drops from 1,980 to 800 feet. The whole approach is densely covered with fiery foliage throughout the late fall. The 4.9-mile West Rim Loop Trail has plenty of boulders along the way for sunning and napping after viewing the park's three gorges. Incredibly, con-

highlight

A Trek for Two

An overnight horseback trip not exotic enough for you? How about leading a llama expedition in the breathtaking Chattahoochee National Forest! You'll enjoy the rustic beauty of this wonderful old forest as you lead a llama carrying all your gear, the fixings for a hearty lunch, and a hammock for an afternoon siesta under a shady tree. Fun, different, and an easy-to-moderate hike. The site is convenient to the Chief Vann House State Historic Site, the 1804 Chatsworth home of Cherokee Nation leader James Vann; Chickamauga Battlefield, Fort Mountain Park, and outlet malls.

**Hawksbell Farm
1618 Dawnville Road
Dalton / 800-208-9008
ext. 7197**

**Chief Vann House State Historic Site
GA Highway 82, 225 N
Chatsworth / 706-695-2598**

sidering the wealth of natural beauty, the park is not heavily visited, making for a secluded visit that can remain your little secret.

🌲 **Cloudland Canyon State Park**
122 Cloudland Canyon Park Road / Rising Fawn / 706-657-4050

A fairly strenuous 0.5-mile trail leads from the parking area to the Brasstown Bald Visitors Center in Union County, but the effort is richly rewarded with a profusion of fall color. Just remember, this is Georgia's highest peak, and fall temperatures are much cooler than those at lower altitudes, so if you forget a sweater you might have to snuggle. On second thought . . .

🌲 **Brasstown Bald Visitors Center**
State Road 180 / Blairsville / 706-896-2556

GARDENS

They are favorite places for the birds and the bees—they might be among your favorite places, too. Touring gardens—whether they are educational botanical gardens or those connected with historic homes—is a natural outing for lovers. The climate and plant matter of Georgia are so varied that, like love itself, a Georgia garden is always in bloom.

Callaway Gardens is among the most romantic destinations in the state. Even the garden's founding grew out of a romantic act. On a drive in the country with his family in the 1930s, textile mogul Cason J. Callaway stopped by the roadside to pick a sprig of bright red wild azalea for his wife. Virginia Callaway was an extremely knowledgeable plantswoman and identified the *prunifolia* or plumleaf azalea as one so rare as to be almost extinct. Callaway responded by buying his beloved wife the land beneath

THE GREAT OUTDOORS 37

the rare plant—and the surrounding 2,500 acres. The family soon built the Blue Spring Farm compound as a weekend getaway and plant sanctuary. Later, when Mrs. Callaway asked for a magnolia tree for her birthday, a truckload of 5,000 arrived. Today, the 14,000-acre garden incorporates a 7.5-mile Discovery Trail circulating among the Day Butterfly Center; the eighteenth-century Pioneer Log Cabin; the Ida Cason Callaway Memorial Chapel; Mr. Cason's Vegetable Garden (the Southern filming site of the Public Broadcasting System's *The Victory Garden*); and the Sibley Horticultural Center; with woods, streams, and lakes dotted throughout. A ferry is available to take riders across Mountain Creek Lake or paddleboats for two can be rented for the same trip.

The Day Butterfly Center, in particular, is a romantic favorite. The 15,000-sq. ft. glass enclosure is the largest conservatory of its kind in North America. Its 1,000 tropical butterflies dance around visitors strolling leisurely through the manicured setting. Some are so tame they will light on an outstretched hand. The tower of the memorial chapel is louvered in such a way that the music from the Moller pipe organ housed inside can be heard throughout the accompanying lawns as well as inside the church. Restaurants from casual to formal, and a variety of lodging in inns and cabins, suit every taste and budget. Pine Mountain itself, located on U.S. 27, is home to many restaurants and the Pine Mountain Antique Mall, a fifty-dealer outlet on Main Street that holds auctions on the second and fourth Saturdays of the month. If there is time left in the day, the 500-acre Wild Animal Safari Park at Pine Mountain houses 300 different kinds of exotic animals, from alligators to zebras, which can be viewed from an open-air "safari bus."

Callaway Gardens
Pine Mountain / 706-663-2281

Pine Mountain Antique Mall
Main Street / Pine Mountain / 706-663-8165

Wild Animal Safari
1300 Oak Grove Road / Pine Mountain / 800-367-2751

Guido Gardens in Metter has sparkling waterfalls, fountains, topiaries, and picturesque gazebos overlooking slow-running brooks. The gardens are also home to the lovely Chapel in the Pines and the broadcast studio home for the *Seeds from the Sower* religious television show.

Guido Gardens
600 North Lewis Street / Metter / 912-685-2222

Oak Hill, the childhood home and gardens of education advocate Martha Berry, has been maintained as one of the most romantic sites in the state. The white-columned 1847 Oak Hill is decorated in the period style Berry favored, and Berry artifacts—from fine nineteenth-century antiques to her Fordson tractor—are on display at the Martha Berry Museum Plantation. But it is the gardens of the plantation which will put you in mind of love. Flagstone and brick walkways meander through a formal garden of daylilies, tea roses, flowering cherry trees, and assorted annuals and perennials. This formality is contrasted with the naturalistic plantings along miles of hillside nature trails and a fernery trail. Following these paths is rewarded by views of a catfish pond and a wildflower meadow. The well-planned mix of plants assures that there is a show of blooms from early spring until frost. The romantic highlight of the 170-acre grounds is the Bridal Walk, a colonnade of simple columns linked by wrought iron supports through which rambling white roses have intertwined themselves. Beneath this ceiling of fragrant petals is an underplanting of daylilies, bearded irises, and annuals bordering a brick pathway. At the end of the path is a shady gazebo.

🌲 **Oak Hill and the Martha Berry Museum**
P.O. Box 490189 / Mount Berry / 800-220-5504
www.berry.edu/oakhill

Rock City Gardens is a fourteen-acre rock garden high atop historic Lookout Mountain in extreme north Georgia. Its lush gardens and unique rock formations (estimated to be 200 million years old) perfectly compliment the view of seven states from Lover's Leap. The natural views are sublime, and the attraction's Fairyland Caverns and Mother Goose Village are fanciful.

🌲 **Rock City Gardens**
1400 Patten Road / Lookout Mountain / 706-820-2531
www.seerockcity.com

The nine-acre Massee Lane Gardens, just south of Fort Valley, is home to the American Camellia Society and boasts what is probably the world's best collection of camellias. This quintessentially Southern flower blooms in chilly weather making the nine-acre Massee Lane Gardens the perfect garden for romantic visits in winter or early spring. Other display gardens include a Japanese and rose garden, as well as an impressive greenhouse.

🌿 **Massee Lane Gardens**
1 Massee Lane / Fort Valley / 912-967-2358

Atlanta is more than a concrete jungle. The following two urban gardens can transport you away from the noise and pulse of the city. The small Cator Woolford Garden is located off one of Atlanta's major streets in the beautiful Druid Hills neighborhood (which provided many of the locations for the movie *Driving Miss Daisy*), but the garden's winding paths and profusion of naturally maintained plants look every bit the country cottage garden. The garden is owned by the Center for Rehabilitation and Education for Adults and Children.

The Atlanta Botanical Gardens is another urban oasis. The gardens' fifteen car-free acres are surrounded by the hubbub of midtown Atlanta, adjacent to a park designed by Frederick Law Olmstead, builder of New York's Central Park. Some walls and steps built for the Cotton States World Exposition of 1891 remain. A variety of gardens from herb knot gardens to Japanese gardens are complemented by the gardens' impressive collection of exotic and rare plants in its soaring glass Dorothy Chapman Fuqua Conservatory. The conservatory houses an impressive collection of exotic tropical plants such as palms, cycads, ferns, orchids, and epiphytes (air plants). Adjacent to the glasshouse is the Desert House which spotlights Old World succulents like lithops (living stones) and welwitschia (a bizarre plant with no living botanical relatives). Perhaps the single most romantic moment I've enjoyed in Atlanta is watching an unexpected snowfall in the Japanese Garden at the Atlanta Botanical Gardens. However, the minimalist design and series of secluded garden "rooms" of the Japanese Garden can be enjoyed in any season.

Cator Woolford Garden
1815 Ponce de Leon Avenue / Atlanta
404-370-1011

The Atlanta Botanical Gardens
1345 Piedmont Avenue / Atlanta
404-876-5859

Another not-to-be-missed garden for lovers in Atlanta is the Robert L. Staton Rose Garden, part of the Fernbank Museum of Natural History. The garden is a memorial to master rosarian Bob Staton, who first established a rose test garden at Fernbank in 1983. The beautifully laid-out and maintained gardens are now home to 1,300 roses, most of which are All-American Rose Selection (AARS) test plants or American Rose Society Award of Excellence Miniature test plants. Staton's favorite flowers, bearing names such as "Garden Party," "Double Delight," and "Olympiad," are specially marked in his honor.

Robert L. Staton Rose Garden
Fernbank Science Center
156 Heaton Park Drive, NE
Atlanta / 404-378-4311

Two sites in Athens are ideal for lovers. The State Botanical Garden of Georgia is a 313-acre preserve set aside by the University of Georgia in 1968. The Garden contains a number of specialized gardens and collections including native Georgia flora, and rare and endangered species; as well as over five miles of nature trails, some of which parallel the Middle Oconee River. A conservatory houses a permanent display of tropical and semi-tropical plants in a gently sloping indoor garden with a trickling waterfall. The garden is located one mile from U.S. Route 441 and approximately three miles from the University of Georgia campus. Admission is free.

during Prohibition. A favorite activity, particularly among bird-watchers, is flat water kayaking. Perfect for the novice kayaker, the site is so sparsely populated with visitors that one can typically be on the water for several hours without seeing another person. The seclusion continues at Melon Bluff's three bed and breakfast facilities: the Ripley Farm, a rustic cottage on the rim of the preserve with two bedrooms with private baths, the Palmyra Plantation, an 1840s cottage set on the tidal river; and Palmyra Barn, a nine-room inn with three romantic suites. Highlights from the Melon Bluff kitchens include oyster roasts and afternoon teas.

Melon Bluff
2999 Island Highway
Midway / 888-246-8188
www.melonbluff.com

The Founders Memorial Garden is located on the 1785 campus of the University of Georgia. This historic house and its outbuildings, built in 1857, once served as the state headquarters of the Garden Club of Georgia. The gardens surrounding the beautifully restored and furnished house are maintained as a memorial to the founders of America's first garden club—the Ladies Garden Club of Athens. The grounds contain a boxwood garden, a sunken formal garden and several informal gardens connected by gravel walks. The garden, located on Lumpkin Street, is a stone's throw from the restaurants and pubs of the quintessential sleepy, little college town.

The State Botanical Garden of Georgia
2450 South Milledge Avenue / Athens / 706-542-1244

The Founders Memorial Garden
South Lumpkin Avenue (on the campus of the University of Georgia) / Athens / 706-542-3631

Wormsloe Historic Site contains the ruins of the fortified home constructed by Noble Jones between 1739 and 1745. A beautiful oak-lined drive leads to a museum, nature trails, and a picnic area.

Wormsloe Historic Site
7601 Skidaway Road / Savannah / 912-353-3023

You can stroll the manicured grounds of the Vines Botanical Gardens in Gwinnett County as you share a double-scoop ice cream cone from the garden's own ice cream parlor and bakery. The Vines Gardens are mature for a garden begun only in the 1970s.

Vines Botanical Gardens
3500 Oak Grove Road / Loganville / 770-466-7532

Barnsley Gardens has a rich and romantic history. Despite warnings from neighboring Cherokees that harm would come to his family if Godfrey Barnsley built his home in the 1840s on a crest of an Adairsville-area hill Native Americans considered sacred, Barnsley constructed a twenty-six-room Italian-style villa on the holy grounds. Woodlands, as it was to be called, was to be the first home in the South with hot and cold running water, indoor toilets, and gas lighting. Godfrey's wife, Julia, never lived to see the home completed and her bereft husband planted the elaborate gardens in her memory. Godfrey Barnsley modeled his estate after the work of landscape architect Andrew Jackson Downing, who designed the grounds of the U.S. Capitol and The White House and who popularized the still-perpetuated English Gardening Landscape movement in America. The villa survived the Civil War, the Barnsley family's financial ruin, and the death of many family members, but was abandoned when a turn-of-the-century tornado ripped the roof off the home. Looted and in ruins the house and grounds were purchased in 1988 by Hubertus and Alexandra Fugger. The romantic ruins were left as they were found, but the memorial gardens have been painstakingly restored with antiques roses, wildflower meadows, and a 120-foot perennial border. Elegant swans glide on the mirror-like pond. The garden is not grand in scale or comprehensive in its collection of plants. It is small and intimate as befits Julia Barnsley's memory. The "Spirits of Barnsley," held annually in October, features scary storytelling among the ruins at the garden. Hayrides, bonfire, and costumed figures abound. It is beyond any doubt one of the most romantic places in Georgia.

🌲 **Barnsley Gardens**
Hill Station Road (off GA Highway 140, just west of Adairsville) / Adairsville / 770-773-7480, ext 32

Elachee Nature Science Center is a 1,200-acre nature preserve on the edge of growing Gainesville. Hiking trails, nature ambles, and interpretive exhibits abound.

Elachee Nature Science Center
2125 Elachee Drive / Gainesville / 404-535-1976

Tours

Share giggles and gooseflesh during "Ghost Talk, Ghost Walk," a ninety-minute walking tours of the haunted sights and spooky happenings of Savannah's old city. Accounts come from Margaret Wayne DeBolt's very popular book, *Savannah Spectres and Other Strange Tales.* The tours leave from John Wesley's monument in Reynolds Square.

"Ghost Talk, Ghost Walk"
Savannah / 912-233-3896

After a day of sightseeing, enjoy the brisk river breeze of a boat tour of Georgia's romantic spots. Curled up in a lover's arms, with a bottle of wine nearby—what could be better? Savannah Riverboat Cruises, aboard the replica riverboat *Savannah River Queen,* offers a variety of brunches, dinners, and moonlight tours with lovers in mind.

Savannah Riverboat Cruises
800-786-6404

The antebellum buffet cruise offered by the Augusta River Boat Cruises is an ideal way to enjoy the charm of this old Southern city. A replica of a nineteenth-century sternwheeler leaves from the Fifth Street dock on Thursday evenings.

Augusta River Boat Cruises
706-722-5020

Theme Parks

Love is a rollercoaster, right? But spending a day at a Georgia theme park is sure to put your romance on the upside. Share some child-like fun together at Six Flags Over Georgia, White Water and American Adventures, Zoo Atlanta, or Wild Adventures. Six Flags boasts the Great American Scream Machine, one of the longest and tallest rollercoasters anywhere in the world, and the Viper, a "shuttle loop" roller coaster which propels riders from zero to sixty miles per hour in six seconds flat. That's sure to get your heart going.

At White Water, twosomes can enjoy a day sunning and float-ing at the "Atlantic Ocean" wave pool or riding down every imag-inable kind of water ride, flume, and toboggan. On Friday nights, "dive-in" movies are shown at the wave pool. Swimmers float and frolic in the gigantic pool as movies are projected onto a huge out-door screen and sound is heard through the PA.

Valdosta's Wild Adventures has exotic animals in 170 acres of natural habitats and carnival rides straight out of your childhood, including the Boomerang, The Plunge, Time Warp, and Swingin' Safari. Hot dogs and ice cream cones will fuel your day of fun.

Spend the day with the birds and the bees—and gorillas, zebras, giraffes, tigers, and polar bears. Zoo Atlanta's excellently designed grounds are perfect for strolling with your special some-one watching, studying, and perhaps even learning something from the animal kingdom about love.

Six Flags Over Georgia
7561 Six Flags Parkway / Austell / 770-739-3400
www.sixflags.com

White Water
250 Cobb Parkway / North Marietta / 770-424-9283

🏫 **Wild Adventures**
3766 Old Clyattville Road (exit 3A of I-75) / Valdosta
800-808-0872 / www.wild-adventure.com

🏫 **Zoo Atlanta**
800 Cherokee Atlanta (off I-20 east of Atlanta in Grant Park)
Atlanta / 404-624-5600

PICNIC SPOTS

Augusta's Riverwalk is a great place to picnic. The main entrance at Eighth and Reynolds streets is marked by a fountain gurgling from the brick-lined plaza. Below the breach in the levee, walkways meander through gardens, playgrounds, and the scenic bulwark which extend over the river. The top of the levee is a flag-lined esplanade with plaques interpreting the area's long history, along with pubs, art galleries, and shops. Along the way you will also see the *Kathryn S. Paddlewheel,* a full-scale model of the last sternwheeler to operate on the Savannah; Fort Discovery/National Science Center; Takurazuka, a waterfall garden given to the people of Augusta by the citizens of its sister city in Japan; and the Morris Museum of Art. A crowded schedule of festivals and special events make Riverwalk a vibrant, exciting destination. Consider a picnic of take-away from Sconyer's Bar-B-Que, a Richmond County favorite since 1956, it was named as one of the nation's top ten barbecue restaurants by *People* magazine.

🏫 **Augusta Riverwalk Information**
706-722-6052

🏫 **Fort Discovery**
Augusta / National Science Center / 706-722-6582

🏫 **Morris Museum of Art**
Augusta / 706-724-7501

Sconyer's Bar-B-Que
2250 Sconyers Way / Augusta / 706-790-5411

Located on the shores of Clark's Hill Lake, Mistletoe State Park is the perfect place for lovers to enjoy a meal outdoors. Miles of nature and hiking trails are shaded by mistletoe-hung trees. The park is a favorite picnic spot so consider ordering a to-go feast from Good To Go in nearby Augusta to enjoy under that romantic canopy of oaks.

Mistletoe State Park
3723 Mistletoe Road / Appling / 706-541-0321

Good To Go
3937 Washington Road / Augusta / 706-854-9400

PICK YOUR OWN

Georgia has an abundance of pick-your-own-fruit farms which make for a wonderful day in the country. Strawberries, peaches, apples, and a variety of berries can be picked in the morning and enjoyed with champagne at night. The list below is selective and includes a variety of favorite farms, both large and small, which have a variety of seasonal crops available throughout the year. For a complete list of pick-your-own farms in Georgia, send a self-addressed stamped envelope to the Georgia Department of Agriculture. The department also oversees seven State Farmers' Markets in Atlanta, Athens, Augusta, Columbus, Macon, Savannah, and Thomasville.

Georgia Department of Argiculture
www.agr.state.ga.us

At Burt's Farm on Georgia Highway 52, just east of Amicalola Falls, a tractor-drawn hay wagon will take you into the Dawson

County pumpkin fields to select your own in season. Pumpkin bread, rolls, pies, and preserves are available—as well as caramel-coated and chocolate- and blueberry-flavored popcorn made from corn grown on the spot. Burt's also makes popcorn meal for cornbread. The annual Appalachian Christmas celebration features a ride on an open wagon (covered in the event of rain or snow) pulled over a covered bridge and through a display of thirty-five seasonal animated scenes made from over 500,000 Christmas lights. Hot chocolate and a bonfire for roasting marshmallows awaits you at the end of the tour.

🌲 **Burt's Farm**
U.S. Highway 52 (near Amicalola Falls) / 800-600-BURT

Double Q Farms specializes in kiwis, but has several other seasonal crops. This Houston County family farm is an area favorite.

🌳 **Double Q Farms**
475 Hwy. 26 / Hawkinsville / 912-892-3794

Fred's Famous Peanuts in Helen sells goobers eight ways to Sunday: boiled, fresh, fried, roasted, or made into brittle and butter. A great way to get to Fred's is to take a shuttle ride with Woody's Mountain Bikes. The company rents mountain bikes at Unicoi Gap State Park for the fourteen-mile ride to the peanut emporium. Along the route, which has several downhill slopes, there are plenty of waterfalls and opportunities to swim in the 'Hooch. After you've arrived at Fred's and had a chance to refuel, employees from Woody's Mountain Bikes (located very near the peanut stand) will shuttle you back to your car at Unicoi Gap. Woody's can also arrange trailside picnics, waterfall sidetrips, and sunset rides according to your fitness level and time specifications.

🌲 **Fred's Famous Peanuts**
17 Clayton Drive / Helen / 706-878-3124

🌲 **Woody's Mountain Bikes**
Highway 356 / Helen / 706-878-3715

Fritchey's Garden is a roadside stand with a variety of fresh veg-
etables, jellies, and honey all year. Pick your own favorite variety
of apples and the staff will make you a fresh apple smoothie on the
spot. Fritchey's sells made-to-order fried fruit and sweet potato
pies. There is an active beehive on site for honey-lovers.

🌲 **Fritchey's Garden**
Batesville / Ga Highway 17 (just before GA Highway 255)

Two Calhoun County pick-your-own farms have a variety of seasonal produce:

🌲 **Payne's Farm**
2259 U.S. Hwy. 41, SW / Calhoun / 706-629-6000

🌲 **Fox Blueberry Farm**
Owens Chapel Road / Calhoun / 706-629-1085

Garmon's Organics is a Carroll County grower of chemical-free
blueberries and muscadine and scuppernong grapes, among other
seasonal crops.

🏘 **Garmon's Organics**
327 Old Four Notch Road / Whitesburg / 770-214-9725

Muscadines are the prize crop of Coweta County's Harrell's Vineyard.

🏘 **Harrell's Vineyard**
4621 W. Hwy. 34 / Newnan & Franklin / 770-251-1507

In the heart of Georgia's apple country, a stand-out orchard is
Panorama Orchards, two miles south of Ellijay. This Gilmer

County farm operates a country-style store to sell its fried pies, apple brandy cake, and caramel apples. A good time to visit this family business, started in 1927 by the Stembridge family, is during the county's annual apple festival, held the second and third weekends of October. Better still, keep in mind that the second weekend in October and the Columbus Day weekend is the date for the annual Prater's Mill Country Fair in nearby Dalton on the site of an 1855 water-powered mill. Events are held in various locations centered around the charming town. Pick up a driving-tour map of the surrounding orchards from the Gilmer County Chamber of Commerce on the town square.

🌲 **Panorama Orchards**
   GA Highway 515 / Ellijay / 706-276-3813

🌲 **Prater's Mill Country Fair**
   Dalton / 706-694-MILL / pratersmill@dalton.net

Hillcrest Orchards offers eighty acres of some twenty varieties of dwarf apple trees which produce apple treats in countless form— ciders, dried apples, Ellijay apple bread, and apple cider doughnuts. The farm, owned by the Reece family since 1946, also produces peaches, sorghum syrup, mountain honey, pumpkins, gourds, Indian corn, strawberries, and homemade ice cream in season. A special attraction at the family farm is the Spooky Trail which features a hay ride from the barn-like store through the orchards to a haunted house with live and animated scary scenes. Beware—some surprises await you among the moonlit trees of the orchard. For scaredy-cats, Hillcrest Orchards also offers a night wagon ride through the farm ending in a roaring bonfire with marshmallows and weenies for roasting.

🌲 **Hillcrest Orchards**
   9696 Highway 52 / Ellijay / 706-273-3838

If you're not in the mood to pick, there are plenty of roadside produce stands dotting Georgia's romantic back roads. Serendipity is
your best guide to finding a special place, but two Georgia stands
are destinations in themselves.

The Carnes family combs their wooded property to collect
strawberries, crabapples, elderberries, and fox and muscadine
grapes to make into organic preserves and jellies. The couple is
best known for their Plum Nutty Spread, a conserve of wild plums,
black walnuts, and oranges sold at their own small store.

🌲 **Carnes' Nectar of the Wild**
Main Street / Clayton / 706-782-5788

🏠 **Dene's General Store**
U.S. Highway 29 / Madras / 770-251-8068

FESTIVALS

The Coosa River Christmas Lighted Boat Parade is a romantic way
to spend a chilly holiday evening. On the first Saturday in
December, the river hosts a floating extravaganza of twinkling
lights, music, and fireworks. The best viewing is from the levee in
downtown Rome. You might start out that romantic evening with
a candlelight tour of the gardens and fernery trail of the nearby
Oak Hill Plantation in Mount Berry.

🏠 **The Coosa River Christmas Lighted Boat Parade**
Rome / 800-444-1834, ext 25

🌲 **Oak Hill Plantation**
P.O. Box 490189 / Mount Berry / 800-220-5504
www.berry.edu/oakhill

People come from all over north Georgia in search of Hot
Thomas-brand peaches in Watkinsville. There is a roadside peach

stand in season that offers other produce as well. The Thomases also run Hot Thomas Barbeque, a must-stop when you're in the Athens area.

Hot Thomas Barbeque & Peach Orchard
3752 Highway 15 (just south of downtown Watkinsville)
Watkinsville / 706-769-6550

The Yellow Daisy Festival celebrates the rare *Viguiera porteri,* a native yellow daisy that blooms in the weathered granite crags of Stone Mountain. The two-and-a-half foot daisies bloom in September and transform the usual gray of the granite outcropping to a vibrant yellow. The event, which happens annually in the second weekend of September, includes the Georgia State Fiddling Championship, buck dancing, flower shows, and an arts and crafts show. The flowers were first identified in 1846 by noted botanist Asa Gray and, outside of Stone Mountain, they can only be found growing in California. Yellow daisies are best enjoyed in the wild—they wilt immediately after they are cut or picked.

Stone Mountain State Park
Highway 78 / Stone Mountain / 800-317-2006

The Cherry Blossom Festival celebrates the abundance of this delicate pink blossom in Macon. There are, in fact, 170,000 Yoshino cherry trees in the city—more than in Washington, D.C., or in any single Japanese town. The first festival was held in 1982 to honor William A. Fickling, who was the first to plant large numbers of the trees in his hometown. His family continues his legacy and plants as many as 10,000 of the trees each year. The festival takes place in late March when the trees are at their showiest and consists of many parades, polo matches, riding exhibitions, and art and antiques shows. Perhaps the romantic highlights of the 200 events are the numerous tours of homes throughout the city's many historic districts. The spring blossoms form a lovely backdrop to the "White Columns Walking Tour."

Macon-Bibb County Convention & Visitors Bureau
912-743-3401

The Powers' Crossroads is one of the oldest and most popular fairs in the state held every Labor Day weekend. Hundreds of artists, local and from surrounding states, offer their wares alongside demonstrations of life in rural Georgia in times gone past.

Powers' Crossroads Country Fair and Arts Festival
Ga Highway 34 (about ten miles south of Newnan)

spotlight

STARGAZING

Viewing a dramatic sunset or studying the midnight stars is romantic wherever you share it together, but following are a few of the best places to catch Mother Nature's nightly show.

Davidson-Arabia Mountain Nature Preserve in Lithonia affords spectacular views toward Atlanta from the many granite outcroppings among its 522 acres of piney woods and wetlands.

Davidson-Arabia Mountain Nature Preserve
3787 Klondike Road / Lithonia / 770-484-3060

The thirty-six-inch telescope at the Fernbank Science Center Observatory is the largest south of Virginia.

Fernbank Science Center
156 Heaton Park Drive / Decatur / 404-378-4314

The panorama of four states from Brasstown Bald, Georgia's highest mountain at 4,784 feet above sea level, is a spectacular view.

Brasstown Bald
State Road 180 / Blairsville / 706-896-2556

Other forms of stargazing are less obvious but just as romantic. The St. Simon's Lighthouse has stood at the tip of St. Simons Island since 1810. The present 104-foot tower is the perfect place to view the setting of the sun.

The Polaris Lounge gives the appearance that a blue-domed space ship has landed atop the Hyatt Regency Atlanta (404-577-1234) at 265 Peachtree Street, NE. This marvel of '70s style gives a magnificent panoramic view of the city, complemented by the house specialties of prime rib and lobster and its extensive wine list. A similarly spectacular 360-degree view is available at the Polaris's across-the-street neighbor, The Westin Peachtree

spotlight

STARGAZING

Plaza. The Sun Dial Restaurant, Bar, and View (404-659-1400) is on the seventy-second floor of North America's tallest hotel, at 210 Peachtree Street, NW. Specializing in hickory-smoked prime rib and featuring jazz nightly, the restaurant is known locally as an ideal setting for marriage proposals.

(The Old Farmer's Almanac gives easy-to-follow and extremely precise charts of the time the sun will set on a given day. Your well-laid plans will be very spontaneous! The online version is available at www.almanac.com/rise/rise.html.)

Play On

We love because it's the only true adventure.—Nikki Giovanni

Two things are sure to get the adrenaline pumping and the heart racing—love and sharing sports together. An added benefit is that you'll live longer and love longer. While the previous chapter gave great ideas on how to share the outdoors together, you may find that your idea of romance leans more toward daredevil thrills or even a little healthy competition. If so, read on and play on. While the romantic notions suggested below are a little more rigorous than those in the previous chapter, you'll find most suggestions fun and easy for even the novice outdoorsperson.

Start from the Chattahoochee Outdoor Nature Center, located in Dunwoody, for a long and lazy float down the Chattahoochee River. The center rents rafts and canoes, life jackets, and paddles, and operates a shuttle service to transport river riders back to their starting points. You are likely to see magnificent native kingfishers along the way. The center has an impressive display of bald eagles and raptors. Various routes and departure points can be selected depending on how long a trip is desired, usually from one to four hours.

Chattahoochee Outdoor Nature Center
1990 Island Ford Parkway / Dunwoody / 404-395-6851
www.vickery.net

UP, UP, AND AWAY

Take an old-fashioned biplane ride for two at Peachtree DeKalb Airport. You can even wear the 1920s-style goggles and leather aviator helmets of Lindbergh and Earhart vintage and fly in an open cockpit PT-17 over downtown Atlanta or buzz Lake Lanier in a World War II-vintage Stearman bi-plane. For those with an iron stomach, Biplanes Over Atlanta will thrill you with aerobatic rides complete with loops, rolls, and spins.

After your flight of fancy, enjoy lunch or dinner at the 57th Fighter Group restaurant just off the grounds of the airport. The restaurant is a stage set of a World War II officers' club inside a farmhouse in the French countryside. The approach to the restaurant is strewn with the burned-out hulks of overturned Jeeps and tanks, and the walls of the entrance to the restaurant have been fortified against Axis attack with sandbags. It is packed with vintage aviation memorabilia and has good views of the planes taking off from the runway. Specialties include prime rib, citrus salmon, rack of lamb Polonaise, and Jack Daniels chicken. The NCO Club, a part of the restaurant, has an outdoor dance floor with a DJ spinning retro hits. A fireplace indoors rounds out the romantic atmosphere.

Biplanes Over Atlanta
Peachtree DeKalb Airport / 2000 Airport Road, Suite106
Chamblee / 770-458-3633 / www.biplanesoveratlanta.com

57th Fighter Group
3829 Clairmont Road / Atlanta / 770-457-7757
http://menus.atlanta.com/57th/index.html

Take your romance to new heights with a hot air balloon ride. Since there is no vibration from machinery or engines once you are aloft, ballooning give a wonderful sense of floating. You can glide across the surface of a lake or graze the tops of trees in intimate quiet.

AdVentures Aloft, located in Helen, gives champagne hot air tours of varying lengths across the North Georgia mountains.

Balloon Safaris International can arrange almost any type of pleasure flight you can imagine anywhere in the state, including sunset tours to your specifications.

AdVentures Aloft
Helen / 770-963-0149

Balloon Safaris International
2868A Lenora Road / Snellville
770-972-1741
balloon@mindspring.com

LOVE ON THE LINKS

Golf and tennis are perfect sports to share. They can certainly be played with cut-throat competitiveness, but can also just be the setting for a day spent enjoying the sunshine and fresh air with someone special. And if your mate leaves you alone every weekend to pursue his or her passion on the links or courts, a getaway vacation is the perfect time to start sharing your lover's interest.

GOLF Digest magazine offers two instruction schools: one at Château Élan in Braselton, another at The Cloister on Sea Island.

The Château Élan school offers two-day weekend packages on its tournament-quality course near the château's vineyard. There is water on ten of the eighteen holes. The school will make recommendations on hotel and bed and breakfast accommodations, or you can stay at The Inn at Château Élan, a French-inspired country inn.

The Sea Island school takes place at the Mobil Five-Star, 1928 Cloister hotel on Sea Island with all the hotel's spa and restaurant facilities nearby. The school is strictly state-of-the-art, complete with multiple-camera video studios, covered practice stations, and simulations of every imaginable green, fairway, and putting situation. Whether to introduce a non-playing partner to the hobby or to share an old pastime, a getaway golf weekend is a lovely way to share time and common interest.

GOLF Digest Instruction Schools
800-243-6121

Château Élan Golf Club
6060 Golf Club Drive / Braselton
404-339-9838 / www.chateauelan.com

The Cloister
Sea Island / 800-732-4752

Sea Island Golf Club
100 Retreat Avenue / St. Simons Island / 912-638-5118

The Renaissance Pine Isle Resort, located at Lake Lanier, is considered by many to be one of the finest golf resorts in the country. Beautifully situated on Lake Lanier, the Pine Isle instructional course offers inspiring views both of the water and the Blue Ridge mountains. If you tire of the links, horseback riding, tennis, and swimming await. Three-day and five-day packages are available.

Renaissance Pine Isle Resort
9000 Holiday Road / Lake Lanier Islands / 770-945-8921

LOVE ALL

Kelly Gunterman Tennis School takes full advantage of the beautiful seaside setting of the Jekyll Island Club Hotel, where highs in the winter average sixty degrees, in spring and fall seventy degrees, and in summer eighty degrees. Mr. Gunterman's teaching philosophy is low-key and pragmatic, and his "Weekend in Georgia" package focuses on common sense techniques and refinements, not reconstruction, of players' games. Fun is emphasized as much as improvement. The hotel offers many activities for twosomes to share after a day at the net: hiking, biking, horseback riding, sailing, beach and poolside lounging, and a full battery of spa services.

Jekyll Island Club Hotel
371 Riverview Drive / Jekyll Island
800-426-3930

The Cloister, located on Sea Island, offers a similar, but perhaps more inclusive program with its three-day "Tennis Package." Accommodations are in the hotel and the package includes three meals a day in The Cloister's acclaimed restaurant. Play is on HarTru clay courts. After a day on the court, you might head for the Sea Island Beach Club Spa to enjoy the services of a fitness trainer, nutritionist, and massage therapist, or you might head for the beach, gym, outdoor pool, or aerobics classes.

The Cloister
Sea Island / 912-638-3611

SADDLED FOR LOVE

Horses have always been associated with romance whether its Heathcliff riding across the moors to his Catherine or the rough riding romance of the Old West. Options abound in Georgia for fun and love on horseback from short excursions to overnight trail rides.

Riders leave the F.D.R. Riding Stables at Franklin D. Roosevelt State Park in Pine Mountain for an overnight ride at around 4:00 P.M. They trek about three miles up a path to the deeply wooded camp site atop Pine Mountain. While the path is steep and sometimes craggy, the inexperienced rider should know that the horses will not gallop on these narrow trails. At the campsite, campers unsaddle and groom their mounts, pitch their tents for the night, and prepare the evening meal, before swapping tall tales and ghost stories around the campfire. It is the closest thing to the dude ranch experience as one's likely to get in Georgia. Trips can be arranged for any length ranging from an afternoon up to five days.

Perhaps the most romantic time for a trip is New Year's Eve, when all the fireworks displays of the valley light up the chilly night sky. If you prefer a shorter trail ride, there is an easy two-mile trail which crosses shallow creeks, or you might simply take a walk along the many nature trails meandering through the farm's eighty acres. One path will lead you to a wooden swing on a knoll in the middle of Turkey Creek, a great place to rest and soak your feet in the stream's cool water. Afterward, camp overnight in one of the farm's twenty tepees, one of which is actually set in its own tiny island in the middle of a small pond and must be approached by a wooden footbridge. You can build a fire right inside your tepee, some of which are large enough to sleep eighteen. (Cabins—with Jacuzzis, stone fireplaces, decks, and spiral staircases—are also available for those who don't want to rough it.) If your weekend schedule allows, go to Butts Mill Farm for its Saturday night barn dance and barbeque dinner. Live music and line dancing are highlights at this restored eighty-acre farm built in the mid-nineteenth-century around a grist mill and cotton gin. The restored mill is found two miles west of Pine Mountain on Butts Mill Road.

F.D.R. Riding Stables
Franklin D. Roosevelt State Park / Box 2970
State Road 190 East / Pine Mountain / 706-628-4533

Butts Mill Farm
P.O. Box 1600 / Butts Mill Road (off U.S. Highway 27)
Pine Mountain / 706-663-7400 (information)
706-663-7007 (reservations) / www.buttsmillfarm.com

The three-day "Ranch, Raft, and Rail" tour offered by the Eagle Adventure Company in McCaysville includes riding in the Cherokee National Forest, whitewater rafting on the Occoee River, and a train ride on the Great Smoky Mountain Railway through the Nantahala River Gorge. Rustic bungalows, cabins, and bed and breakfast inns provide lodging along the way.

Eagle Adventure Company
P.O. Box 970 / McCaysville / 800-288-3245

Have some down-home fun—a-kissin' and a-neckin' on a hayride. Sweet Sunshine Equestrian Center has old-fashioned, get-lost-in-a-haystack hayrides in addition to wonderful trail rides. (At the center is the Sunshine Petting Zoo, which is the home of GOGO the Goat, co-star of *The Rudy and GOGO World Famous Cartoon Show*.) Sweet Sunshine is located three miles from Crabapple in Alpharetta. After your ride, enjoy an iced tea and lunch at Mr. John B's Restaurant, a local favorite nestled in a cluster of antique shops. The

Gold City Corral, located at the Forrest Hill Mountain Hideaway Resort has a romantic dinner and wagon tour package aboard a rustic Amish-style farm wagon pulled by mules or Belgian horses, as well as carriage rides in which a vintage white Visa-Vee carriage is pulled by a team of Belgian horses.

Sweet Sunshine Equestrian Center
14295 Birmingham Highway / Alpharetta
770-343-9807

Mr. John B's Restaurant
780 Mayfield Road / Crabapple / 770-751-7381

Gold City Corral
Forrest Hill Mountain Hideaway Resort
135 Forrest Hill Drive / Dahlonega
706-864-6456 / dkraft@stc.net

BICYCLING TOURS MADE FOR TWO

Callaway Gardens Resort, located in Pine Mountain, offers the 7.5-mile Discovery Bicycle Trail through the garden's woodland areas. Begin at the Bike Barn (rentals are available) and meander past the Day Butterfly Center, chapel, historical vegetable garden, and various streams and lakes. You'll see rare azaleas, native to and grown only in a 100-mile radius of the center. At the end of the trail, a ferry will whisk you across Mountain Creek Lake back to the starting point.

Callaway Gardens
Pine Mountain / 706-663-2281

Take a swing through the swamp. The Okefenokee Swamp, part of the Okefenokee National Wildlife Refuge in Folkston, Charlton County, is not at all as harsh or stark as the word "swamp" is commonly conceived. One of the oldest and best-preserved fresh-water areas in America, it is actually a beautiful, tranquil wetland bog of watery forest and mammoth, Spanish moss-draped cypresses. Begin at the parking area of the Visitors Center for the beautiful 8.2-mile ride. You'll see wading birds, dozens of species of songbirds, and a forest of loblolly, bay, and heart pine trees. The black water swamp looks wonderfully ancient and untouched (the water is said to be ninety-eight per cent pure), but modern conveniences (a photographer's blind, an observation tower, and restrooms) dot the trail. Consider scheduling your trip to coincide with either of two fun local events: the Loose Caboose Street Dance (third week in June), or the Okefenokee Festival (second weekend in October).

U.S. Fish and Wildlife Service
Okefenokee National Wildlife Refuge / Route 2, Box 3330
Folkston / 912-496-3331

Biking is the perfect way to share the natural charm and historical pleasures of the Augusta Canal bike trails, formerly the old tow-path where mules pulled barges up and down the waterway. Greeneway and Turkey Creek lead around the nine-mile canal constructed in 1846. Meander along the strip of land separating the canal from the Savannah River or circle Warren and Olmstead lakes, connected to the canal, before heading to the levee, part of Riverwalk. Riverwalk is a waterfront development that incorporates some National Register of Historic Places with restaurants and pubs perfect for satisfying your post-ride appetite.

Augusta Canal Authority
P.O. Box 2367 / Augusta / 706-823-0440
www.augustacanal.com

HIKING

After a beautiful hike or trail ride in Red Top Mountain State Park
in Cartersville, enjoy a dinner in the lodge dining room at which
you'll see wild deer feeding from troughs outside the large windows. The annual arts festival is a popular draw. Be sure to take
empty jugs to collect the pure, fresh-tasting water for which
nearby Cave Spring is famous. The park is located off exit 123 of
I-75 in Cartersville and is surrounded on three sides by the man-
made Lake Allatoona.

Red Top Mountain State Park
653 Red Top Mountain, SE / Cartersville / 770-975-0055

Considered one of the state's seven wonders, 1,108-acre Providence
Canyon is also known as Georgia's "Little Grand Canyon." One of
the most romantic sights in the state is the full moon rising over the
canyon, viewed from one of Providence Canyon Conservation
Park's six reservable primitive campsites.

Providence Canyon Conservation Park
Route 1, Box 158 / State Highway 39C / Lumpkin
912-838-6202 (information) / 800-864-7275 (reservations)

If you and your loved one are getting along swimmingly, the natural thing to do is enjoy a day on the water together.

Enjoy one of Georgia's most beautiful waterways, the historic
Augusta Canal, while you help the community. The Augusta Canal
Canoe Cruise and Barbeque Cookout is an annual fundraiser for
Peach State 90.7 Public Radio. After a leisurely, seven-mile paddle
and float from the old city locks to the heart of the Garden City,
enjoy some of the South's best barbeque and live music at lovely
Meadow Garden. Canoe rental is available on the Savannah River.

Augusta Canal Authority
P.O. Box 2367 / Augusta / 888-659-8926 / www.augustacanal.com

The Flint River is a wonderful, undeveloped river perfect for a quiet canoe paddle tour for two, as well as for guided raft rides. The Canoe the Flint company offers guided and unguided tours leaving from Thomaston.

Canoe the Flint
4429 Woodland Road / State Road 36 at Flint River
Thomaston / 404-647-2633

The "Saddle and Paddle" tour, offered by Southeastern Expeditions in Atlanta and Sunburst Stables in Clarkesville, is a full day of whitewater rafting on the Chattooga River, followed by a three-hour horseback ride through the Chattahoochee National Forest, and concluding with a one- or two-night stay in Sunburst's private, hot tub- and fireplace-equipped cabins. The packages are priced per couple. The company also arranges whitewater tours that combine the best of both worlds: the rustic beauty of rafting on the Chattooga and the charm of accommodations at one of Georgia's most celebrated bed and breakfasts, the Glen Ella Inn in Clarkesville. Although the rafting is overseen by the experts at Southeastern Expeditions, the package is arranged by the inn.

Southeastern Expeditions
50 Executive Park South, Suite 5016 / Atlanta / 800-868-7238

Glen Ella Inn and Conference Center
1789 Bear Gap Road / Clarkesville / 888-455-8893

SNOW SKIING

Snow skiing in the Peach State? Why, yes, at the Sky Valley Resort, the state's only ski slope. From mid-December to mid-March, whenever the temperature drops to around freezing, the snow-making equipment is juiced up along the resort's four slopes and bunny hill. Snowboarding and night skiing are added for extra fun. If the powder isn't to your liking, skip directly to après-ski snuggling in the lodge with your loved one.

🌲 **Sky Valley Resort**
   One Sky Valley Way / Sky Valley / 706-746-5301

Got a Brand-New Pair of Roller Skates

Skate Escape, directly across from Piedmont Park, midtown Atlanta's equivalent of Central Park, rents inline skates. Take them across the street to tour the wide paved trails around Lake Claire, the Bathhouse, and the Isamu Naguchi-designed playground. Afterward, get a bite to eat on the casual veranda of Einstein's or any number of restaurants near Piedmont Avenue and Tenth Street, or along Juniper Street near Fourteenth Street, all easy walks from the park.

🏃 **Skate Escape**
   1086 Piedmont Avenue, NE / Atlanta / 404-892-292

🏃 **Einstein's**
   1077 Juniper Street / Atlanta / 404-876-7925

Magic Mountains

One word frees us of all the weight and pain of life: that word is love.—*Sophocles*

There are abundant natural wonders to be found in northeast Georgia—not the least of which are many couples celebrating their love. The pristine mountains of the "Empire State of the South" offer activities for any time of the year—wildflower walks in the blush of spring, peaceful escapes from the crush of city summers, foliage hikes in the nip of autumn, and snuggling in front of the fireplace in a snowbound mountain inn. Following are ideas perfect for a mountain getaway.

WATERFALLS

The North Georgia mountains are the home to some breathtaking waterfalls. Following are some lovers' favorites. Visits during the late fall and early spring, especially after heavy rains and the melting of winter snows, are rewarded with the most spectacular shows.

"Amicalola" is Cherokee for "tumbling waters" and so they do at Amicalola Falls, the highest waterfall east of the Mississippi River. Crisp mountain water drops 729 feet through seven cascades—through the upper section in free fall and in the middle and lower portions through a gurgling creek. To see one of the "seven wonders of Georgia," take Highway 52 west from Dahlonega to Amicalola State Park.

Anna Ruby Falls was formed where Curtis Creek and York Creek join in a tumbling, foaming glory in well-loved Unicoi State Park. Asphalt paths lead to two observation decks from which the fifty-foot and 153-foot columns of water can be viewed. When the sun is situated just so overhead, Anna Ruby Falls puts on a show of bright rainbows across the taller York Creek cascade. To visit this impressive natural display, take Georgia 75 north through Helen to the Robertstown Community. Once there, turn right onto Georgia 356 toward Unicoi State Park. After 1.3 miles on Georgia 356, turn left at the Anna Ruby Falls sign. Since Unicoi is among the most visited sites in Georgia, lovers who crave privacy might want to schedule their visit during the week—and everyone should heed the posted advice on the wildflower trail to "take only photographs and leave only footprints."

Three falls—the Becky Branch, Dick's Creek, and Martin Creek falls—are nestled so close together in the north Georgia mountains that they can all be visited in a day's leisurely drive. Located in the Warwoman Dell area, just east of Clayton, Becky Branch Falls can be reached by traveling Highway 441 toward Clayton. Go east on Warwoman Road (County Road 5) for three miles to Poll Creek Road. Parking is on the left side of the road by a small creek. A clearly marked trail on the right side of the creek leads to 200 yards of trail and the base of the falls. To reach Dick's Creek Falls, travel six miles east along Warwoman Road after the junction with Highway 441. Turn right after the Antioch Church onto Dick's Creek Road. Travel one-half mile along Dick's Creek. Take the left across the creek and go three and one-half miles to the second ford. Cross the ford and park near the Bartram National Recreation Trail sign. Follow the trail north to Dick's Creek and follow the rambling trail to the top of the falls. A trail leads downstream about 100 yards to the base of the falls where it empties—in a splendor of light and foam—into the Chattooga River. To round out the daytrip, visit Martin Creek Falls by going east on Warwoman Road for about three miles outside of Clayton until you come to Martin Creek Road. Follow this windy mountain road for another half mile to the creek itself. Walk up the west side of the stream. Surprise—Martin Creek Falls is a series of three falls all producing a wonderful show of prismatic light and relaxing sound.

Minnehaha Falls, just south of Lake Burton in Rabun County, is located at the end of a trail lined with white pine, rhododendron, and thickets of mountain laurel. The waters of Joe Creek fall through shoaling cascades and rock ledges for approximately fifty-five feet of "laughing water," hence the Cherokee name "Minnehaha." Near the base of the higher fall a large boulder is easily reached as a resting or picnic place. Travel to what is arguably the most beautiful of Georgia's falls by taking U.S. 441 from Clayton, then following Lake Rabun Road west around the north end of the lake. Turn left one mile after Rabun Beach Recreation Area. After crossing a small bridge, follow Bear Gap Road around the lake for one and one-half miles. The trail marked Fall Branch Trail will provide an easy hike to the falls. Nearby Angel Falls and Panther Falls, at the northern end of Lake Rabun, are also impressive, but the approach trail is for experienced hikers only.

The two waterfalls that make up High Shoals Falls are truly spectacular—a 100-foot cascade of exuberant liquid light. To get to the falls from Helen, take Georgia Highway 17/75 for approximately 11.4 miles, turning onto Indian Grave Gap Road, F.S. 283 to the High Shoals Scenic Area.

Nineteen feet taller than that generations-old honeymoon destination, Niagra Falls, Georgia's own Toccoa Falls are certainly awe-inspiring. A stream winds its lazy way through the lower portion of the 1,100-acre Toccoa Falls College campus at the base of the 186-foot falls. Located just off Highway 17 north of Toccoa in Stephens County. Follow the signs to the campus.

The 150-foot Dukes Creek Falls boasts a slippery-rock slide and a newly built observation deck. Lovers with mobility limitations will be pleased to find the trail handicap accessible to the first overlook. In the middle of the wide waterfall, several hemlocks and rhododendron cling to a granite outcropping, and below the fall the water collects into a canyon and, finally, Dukes Creek. From Helen, take Georgia 75 north about 1.4 miles to the junction of GA 356 West and Alternate 75. At the bridge, cross the Chattachoochee River and continue for approximately 2.2 miles to the Richard Russell Scenic Highway (Forest Service Road 348). Turn right and travel two miles to the Dukes Creek Falls Recreation Area.

The trail leading to Horse Trough Falls is close to the source spring of the Chattahoochee, what the Cherokee called "the river of the painted rocks." Especially suited to novice hikers, the section of the Appalachian Trail leading to the fall offers beautiful forest, trout streams, and varied wildlife. Horse Trough Falls is not a dramatic freefall, it is instead a surprisingly powerful flume, as remarkable for its thrilling roar as for its visual loveliness.

Helton Creek Falls should be noted, not only for the beauty of the two falls, but because they are among the most easily accessed of the north Georgia waterfalls, an important consideration for the handicapped. An easy 0.2-mile walk—flanked by an allee of hemlocks—from the parking area allows a spectacular view of the larger upper falls. Both falls end in a reflective, dark green pool. The falls are reached by Helton Creek Road and Forest Service Road 118, one and one-half miles north of Neel's Gap, off U.S. Highway 19/129.

DeSoto Falls is a series of five falls located within a three-mile section of the DeSoto Falls Trail. The names derives from a legend that a piece of armor was found near the falls and was purported to have belonged to Hernando DeSoto or one of his troops. A round trip to see the three most-visited cascades is 3.7 miles. To get to the 650-acre scenic area and falls, begin at the intersection of GA 52 and GA 60 with 129, two blocks east of the old Courthouse in Dahlonega. Go north on U.S. 19, two blocks east on 60, for 9.2 miles. Then proceed north on U.S. 19/129 for 4.3 miles. The entrance to the area is on the left.

TUBING AND RAFTING

Put yourself on autopilot and enjoy a leisurely float down Georgia's best tubing river, the Chattahoochee. A river float is a day full of sunshine and cloud-watching—and quiet enough to talk and day-dream together. Cool River, Flea Market Tubing, and Alpine Tubing, all located in Helen, offer approximately two-to-three-hour trips down various stretches of the 'Hooch.

🌲 **Cool River**
Helen / 706-878-2665

🌲 **Flea Market Tubing**
Helen / 706-878-1082

🌲 **Alpine Tubing**
Helen / 706-878-1082

The Amicalola River Rafting Outpost offers rafting, canoeing, tubing, and kayaking down the gently tumbling waters of the Amicalola River. The course of the river winds through a wildlife area on a two-hour trip with an east three-foot drop. The trail is unintimidating for the novice outdoorsperson, yet scenic enough for Grizzly Adams. The Outpost also organizes early morning rafting, canoeing, and kayaking trips though a ten-mile section of the upper Amicalola for the more adventuresome. (Here, too, the drop is a mild one—one five-feet overall.) The Outpost's third package is a trip along a Class IV rapid with an eighty-feet-per-mile drop called, the Edge of the World. Overnight trips on the river can also be arranged, including teepee camping with Native American guides, storytellers, singers, and drummers. ARRO rents mountain cabins which are charmingly rustic on the outside, but equipped with woodstoves, full kitchens, TVs, VCRs, stereos, outdoor grills, hot tubs, and wraparound decks which overlook tree-bordered catfish ponds. ARRO is about six miles west of the 22,000-acre Dawsonville Wildlife Management Area.

🌲 **Amicalola River Rafting Outpost**
706-265-6892

The Broad River in northeast Georgia is one of the state's best (and most-guarded secrets). No doubt, inclusion in a book such as this will make many "locals" groan but, nonetheless, this secluded and scenic river is both breathtaking and romantic. The Broad River Outpost rents kayaks and canoes as well as providing shuttle service.

🏕 **Broad River Outpost**
Wildcat Bridge Road / Daniellsville / 706-795-3242

MOUNTAIN INNS

The word "unique" is used too often, but the Len Foote Hike Inn in Amicola Falls State Park deserves that distinction. The twenty-one-room inn is accessible only by an easy five-mile hike through the Chattahoochee National Forest from the nearest access road. (The handicapped are invited to drive a scenic route with an inn ranger.) The moderate hike is rewarded by the sight of the gray-stained, multi-gabled lodge inspired by the low profile of ancient Japanese rural residences. It appears little more than a nook at the end of Amicola Ridge surrounded by dense hardwood forest, four and one-half miles from Springer Mountain, the southern terminus of the Appalachian Trail. The inn, opened in 1998 and operated by the non-profit Appalachian Education and Recreation Services, will sponsor environmental workshops and nature study meetings as befits a lodge named after Georgia's best-known conservationist of this century, Len Foote (1918–1989). Foote was the inspiration for the Mark Trail comic strip. The lodge has one rule which is strictly enforced: no beepers, cell phones, or laptops are allowed. Reservations are required and accepted up to eleven months in advance.

🌲 **The Len Foote Hike Inn**
Amicalola Falls State Park
770-389-7275 or 800-864-7275

The Cohutta Lodge and Restaurant is secluded on a mountaintop, ten miles from the nearest town of Chatsworth, in an area rich in Native American history. Simple outdoor pleasures—horseshoes, horseback riding, and miniature golf—balance the romantic pleasures of the lodge-secluded woodland cottages and romantic dinners in front of the lodge's stone fireplace. The lodge is convenient to Fort Mountain State Park's mysterious wall of piled stones left by Native Americans, the purpose of which is unknown; the spectacular wilderness view at Cohutta Overlook; and Georgia's deepest lake, Carters Lake.

highlight

Lovers' Sad Tale

The tranquil valleys of the Nacoochee and Sautee were once the setting of a tragic love story. A Cherokee princess, Nacoochee, fell in love at first sight with Sautee, son of an enemy Chickasaw chief. Forbidden to marry, they fled to Yonah Mountain. When he learned of their escape, Nacoochee's enraged father sent warriors to retrieve his daughter. When the warriors found the couple they threw Sautee off a cliff. Nacoochee followed her beloved, jumping to her death. Her grief-stricken father buried the two lovers in a mound at the conjuncture of the two valleys.

🌲 **Cohutta Lodge and Restaurant**
500 Cochise Trail / Chatsworth / 706-695-9601

Forest Hills Mountain Hideaway, located in Dahlonega, is a compound of thirty cabins decorated in styles ranging from the rustic to the frou-frou Victorian. Innkeepers have tried to second guess their guests' every romantic need. In addition to several packages which include such amenities as a souvenir photo, candlelit dinners, and video rentals, a menu of pampering extras is available which ranges from prepared picnic lunches to delivery of candles, champagne flutes, and bubble bath to one's room. Other fun activities include therapeutic massages performed in one's own cabin, renting mountain bikes to tour the nearby Appalachian Trail, and a wagon ride to a candlelit dinner at the nearby Riverhouse restaurant.

🌲 **Forest Hills Mountain Hideaway**
135 Forrest Hills Road / Dahlonega
706-864-6456 or 800-654-6313 / www.foresths.com

Close to Anna Ruby Falls and the many scenic wonders of north Georgia, Unicoi State Park is a destination in itself. The state park offers a 100-room lodge and cabins galore. The Barrel Cottages are so called because of their unique construction from gigantic pipe sections—the two-story rustic cabins do indeed resemble barrels turned on their side. The first floor has a small living room with a wood-burning stove and complete kitchen, and the upstairs has a bedroom with two double beds and a bath. The "barrels" are surrounded by a high wooden deck and nestled under the dense canopy of trees around the fifty-three-acre lake which give the cabins a cozy Swiss Family Robinson feel.

🌲 **Unicoi State Park**
P.O. Box 849 / Helen / 706-878-2201 or 800-864-7275

With its spectacular views of the mountains of Georgia, North Carolina, and Tennessee, as well as its panoramic vistas of the finger lakes of Lake Chatuge, it's no wonder innkeepers Yolanda and David Keating call their mountaintop lodge the Mountain Memories Inn. Located in Hiawassee, several of the six rooms boast two-person showers and poster beds. All rooms are indulgently equipped with Jacuzzis and one has a stone hearth fireplace. Guests are invited on a nightly complimentary boat cruise on Lake Chatuge.

🌲 **The Mountain Memories Inn**
   385 Chancey Drive / Hiawassee / 800-335-VIEW
   www.yhc.edu/users/mtnmem/

If antebellum luxury is more your style, several fine old homes have been renovated as mountain retreats. A white-columned 1848 mansion in Dillard has found new life as the White Hall Inn.

🌲 **White Hall Inn**
   485 Carolina Street / Dillard / 706-746-5511

Located off a gravel road amidst seventeen acres of meadow, gardens, and nature trails, Glen Ella Springs Inn is a delightful retreat. The inn is housed in a turn-of-the-century house painstakingly renovated in 1987, listed on the National Register of Historic Places, and decorated with an impressive selection of antique and vintage furniture. Glen Ella boasts a beautiful herb garden and peaceful wood views. The inn's restaurant is famous for its selection of scones and muffins for breakfast, light fare for lunch, and Creole cuisine for dinner—so much so that discerning diners from Atlanta will gladly make the two-hour drive. The inn sponsors special events like wine tastings, mystery weekends, and herb gardening conferences. Glen Ella has a pool surrounded by a large sun deck and flower gardens. The perfect place to find a keepsake of your mountain getaway is at the Mark of the Potter, also in Clarkesville. The shop sells handmade contemporary crafts including jewelry, textiles, blown glass, and pottery from more than forty regional artists and craftspeople. The Mark of the Potter has operated since 1969 in the converted Grandpa Watts' Grist Mill on the Soque River. Shoppers can feed the shop's "pet" mountain trout as they school under the porch of the 1931 mill, which is cantilevered over the river.

Glen Ella Springs Inn
Bear Gap Road / Clarkesville / 706-754-7295 or 800-552-3479

The Mark of the Potter
GA 197, Route 3 / Clarkesville / 706-947-3440

Herbs for the restaurant at the Inn at Lofty Branch are raised in the inn's own garden. Breakfasts include fresh fruit, omelettes, and freshly baked breads. Rooms feature stacked rock fireplaces. The inn is close to a small cluster of unique shops, including a pottery studio and an organic lunch café called the Green Salamander, set just off U.S. Highway 441 north of Tallulah Falls.

Inn at Lofty Branch
88 Lofty Branch Lane / Lofty Branch / 706-782-3723

There are mountains in Georgia in addition to those we most commonly think of in the north of the state. The cottages at Franklin D. Roosevelt State Park in Pine Mountain—part of a small range cutting through central Georgia—are as beautiful and romantically secluded as they are affordably priced. The older cottages, built with Civilian Conservation Corps labor in the 1930s, have floor-to-ceiling stacked stone fireplaces and are the most desirable. Hiking and fishing around Lake Delano are favorite activities at the park and Callaway Gardens, F.D.R.'s Little White House, and the amenities of the city of Columbus are nearby.

Be sure to visit K. Derum Cabinetmaker in nearby Pine Mountain Valley for a prized souvenir of your trip to the mountains. The fourth generation Latvian cabinetmaker, descended from craftsmen who once made furniture for the Russian nobility, now makes exquisite birdhouses his family business. All the firm's birdhouses are modeled after vernacular forms of Georgia architecture and are named after the regions which inspired them: Warm Springs, Brookstone, Athens, Atlanta, and St. Simons Island.

Franklin D. Roosevelt State Park
Box 2970, Highway 190E / Pine Mountain / 706-663-4858

Lake Lanier is one of the premier destinations in northeast Georgia, and the most romantic way to spend time there is onboard a luxury houseboat. Common houseboat rentals include those which sleep up to ten and come with spacious galleries and roof-top sun decks. Bring along all the essentials for a candlelit dinner or a concert at Lanierland and you'll make special memories. Several companies rent boats by the day or week. Forever Resorts, operating out of Holiday Marina, rents luxury houseboats. Lake Lanier Island Rentals and Harbor Landing are both good rental sources located on Lake Lanier Islands.

Forever Resorts
770-271-5705

Lake Lanier Island Rentals
770-932-7200

Harbor Landing
770-932-7255

GOLF

The 7,030-yard layout of the Château Élan Golf Club winds around lakes and creeks manicured with azalea bushes and dogwood trees. The gently sloping fairways of the original course are punctuated by eighty-seven bunkers, leaving precious little margin of error for bad strategy off the tee. Two other courses complete the club. The course is located beside a "château" with restaurants and a spa on the grounds of the Château Élan Winery.

Château Élan Golf Club
6060 Golf Club Drive / Braselton
770-271-6051 or 800-233-WINE (9463)
www.chateauelan.com / chateau@chateauelan.com

Adjacent to the Igls Resort Villas, the Innsbruck Resort and Golf Club is inspired in design and architecture by lodges of the Austrian Alps. The course, consistently ranked as one of the state's best, is sited among beautiful hills and affords wonderful views of the north Georgia mountains. As befits its Alpine design, several holes have drops and hills, making for challenging play.

Innsbruck Resort and Golf Club
Bahn Innsbruck / Helen / 706-878-2100

The Renaissance Pine Isle Resort looks more woodland than golf course at times-fairways snake alongside and through pine forests and the banks of Lake Lanier to make play as beautiful as it is challenging. The resort has earned a Mobil 4-Star/AAA-4 Diamond rating.

Renaissance Pine Isle Resort
9000 Holiday Road / Lake Lanier Islands / 770-945-8921

spotlight

MITTIE'S WEDDING

Touring the Roswell landmark Bulloch Hall is always romantic. The white-columned Greek Revival was built of heart pine in 1840 by Major James Stephens Bulloch, grandson of Georgia Governor Archibald Bulloch. The major took as much care in the planning of the gardens as he did in the design of the "four-square" house with its eleven fireplaces, pedimented portico, and kitchen with beehive-style oven. For example, because he knew Osage orange trees discourage flies and rodents, Bulloch was careful to plant many of those trees near the house. Today the grounds boast 142 trees on the National Historic Tree Register. Those beautiful grounds are open to the public now as is the house which features many music, literary, and art programs, the most popular of which is probably the spring quilt show.

Bulloch Hall's architectural significance is highlighted by an important romantic footnote. The major's daughter, Martha (known as "Mittie"), was married to a well-off, but little-known man at her family home on December 22, 1853. Mittie's long and happy marriage to Theodore Roosevelt Sr. produced U.S. President Theodore Roosevelt and another son who was the father of Eleanor Roosevelt, wife of Franklin D. Roosevelt. Each year around Christmas time, Mittie's and Theodore's marriage is reenacted in period style in the beautifully maintained home. Bulloch Hall is located one block west of the historic Roswell town square.

spotlight

MITTIE'S WEDDING

There is more to see in Roswell, so consider making a romantic day of it by taking a tour of the nineteenth century city's landmarks. Walking tours are conducted by the Roswell Historical Society (770-992-1665) every Saturday, leaving from the Roswell Visitors Center on the corner of Mimosa and Bulloch avenues; and tours of antebellum Roswell are conducted by Atlanta Discovery Tours (770-667-1414). Settle in for the night at Ten Fifty Canton Street Bed and Breakfast (1050 Canton Street, 770-998-1050), a late-1800s inn within easy walking distance of all the shops, restaurants, and galleries of old Roswell.

Bulloch Hall
180 Bulloch Avenue / Roswell / 770-992-1731

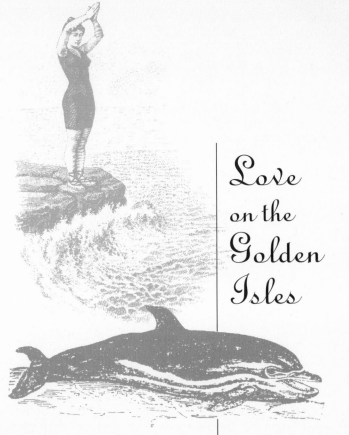

*Love
on the
Golden
Isles*

The love we give away is the only love we keep.—*Elbert Hubbard*

When the sun dips below the horizon and reflects its golden light on the sands and marshes of Georgia's barrier islands, one can only describe them as Golden Isles. The nickname perfectly describes the fifteen islands that make up the chain—Tybee, Skidaway, Little Tybee, Wassaw, Ossabaw, St. Catherines, Blackbeard, Sapelo, Wolf, Little St. Simons, Sea Island, St. Simons, Jekyll, Little Cumberland, and Cumberland. These last six lie amidst one of the world's great tidal estuaries. A lovers' tour of this lovely, romantic stretch of coast should begin with the charm of the port of Savannah and before proceeding to any or all of the barrier islands. Perhaps the best known of the chain are Jekyll and St. Simons, very different from each other, but more different still from the variety of undeveloped lesser-known islands. A couple can find their own island retreat to satisfy whatever romantic mood they require—the down-home welcome of Sapelo, the pampering playground of Sea Island, or the serene solitude of Cumberland.

SAVANNAH

A visit to Savannah is the perfect romantic prelude to the seclusion of a Golden Isle getaway. This Southern belle of a city is

Tidings of Joy

*The Blessing of the Fleet is an old
Darien tradition that is as romantic as it is uplifting and fun.
Darien is the second-oldest
planned town in Georgia and was
established under James
Oglethorpe in 1736. The town's
squares are bejeweled by ancient
live oaks and are situated overlooking the Darien River from a
high bluff. Every spring the traditional blessing of the town's shrimp
fleet occurs, a custom introduced
by the town's earlier
Mediterranean settlers. The event
serves as a sort of town homecom-
ing as local clergy offer prayers
for the McIntosh County fleet's
safety and success over a boat
parade of freshly painted and decorated trawlers. Cheering thousands line the waterfront around
the Darien River Bridge. The festival includes music, arts and
crafts, local seafood, and dancing.
The event is carefully scheduled in
March, April, or May to coincide
with a high tide on Sunday.*

**Darien Chamber of
Commerce
912-437-4192**

located on the Georgia-South Carolina
border, a part of the balmy Low Country
immortalized in Pat Conroy's *Prince of
Tides*. Savannah's history of sophisticated affluence dating to its founding in
1733, the hustle and bustle of its port,
and its recent popularity among fans of
John Berendt's *Midnight in the Garden of
Good and Evil*, make it a vibrant and
lively place to visit. There is so much to
see and do in this city that such a topic
could easily fill the pages of a book in
itself. Start by contacting the Savannah
Convention and Visitor's Bureau for a
complete welcome package of the entic-
ing hospitality that the city has to offer.

Walk hand in hand along River Street,
cobblestoned with stones that were once
ballast in ships visiting the city's port,
and indulge in some shopping. Dine in
restaurants housed in lovingly renovated nineteenth-century "King Cotton"
warehouses along this historic street in
Georgia's founding city. Or enjoy First
Saturday on the Waterfront, a monthly
all-day and all-night street party, often
seasonally themed, on the Riverfront
Plaza featuring arts and crafts, live entertainment, and great food.

Savannah lives up to its reputation as
a party town and its celebration of St.
Patrick' Day, dating back to 1824, is a

doozy—New York's St. Patrick's Day parade and New Orleans' Mardi Gras rolled into one. The whole city becomes a street party and the green beer flows and flows.

Tour the live oak-canopied monuments and time-worn memorials of Bonaventure Cemetery, located just off Pennsylvania Road on Bonaventure Road. Eat at The Times on Bay, with its fine American cuisine in General William Tecumseh Sherman's 1864 military headquarters. The Olde Pink House is another restaurant which easily earns Cupid's Seal of Approval. Located in a stately 1791 mansion, this popular restaurant features three-course dinners of local specialties—sherry-laced she-crab soup, for example. For Southern comfort food served family style, enjoy Mrs. Wilke's Boarding House. Emma "The Lady of 6,000 Songs" Kelly, immortalized in *Midnight* performs standards, show tunes, and torch songs at Hannah's East at the Pirate's House. July is the annual Savannah International Beer, Music, and Food Festival at the Historic Roundhouse. The brewfest features as many as 150 domestic and imported ales, stouts, lagers, pilsners, and specialty brews. Call Bear Foot Sports for more information about schedules.

John Berendt's bestselling story of murderous jealousy and eccentric aristocrats, *Midnight in the Garden of Good and Evil,* has proved such a *succès de scandale* that numerous tours of the houses, watering holes, and locales that inspired the novel have sprung up in the city. One of the best to retrace the steps of the characters in "The Book," as it is called in Savannah, is simply called "The Book" Tour. For a more traditional horse-drawn carriage tours of the city, call Carriage Tours of Savannah. Tours leave from the city's Visitor's Center.

If you'd like a souvenir of your "Book" tour, Southern Images Gallery Street sells posters of Jack Leigh's well-known book cover image of a grave in Bonaventure Cemetery. The statue itself, locally called the Bird Girl, one of three copies of Sylvia Shaw

Judson's 1938 original sculpted as a garden fountain, was purchased for a family plot by Savannahian Lucy Boyd Trosdal. Due to the crush of traffic to Bonaventure to visit the grave site, the family had the Bird Girl removed in 1995 from her serence perch overlooking the Wilmington River. She is now on long-term loan at the Telfair Museum of Art.

If there are Girl Scouts in your family, or someone special is a former Girl Scout, stop by the Juliette Gordon Low Birthplace and Museum when in Savannah. Low founded the Girl Scouts in the city in 1915.

The Juliette Gordon Low Birthplace and Museum
142 Bull Street / Savannah / 912-233-4501

A city as richly historical as Savannah is bound to have urban myths and otherworldly stories. Savannah's ghost tales and history of voodoo and witchcraft are recounted in the Savannah Shadows Ghost Tour, which provides a candlelit walking tour departing from Colonial Park Cemetery. Haunting Tours bring shivers to the spine in its tours of Colonial Park Cemetery and surrounding squares. Old Savannah Tours offers a similar "Ghost Tour" by trolley departing from the Visitors Center. After your tours of the historic district by trolley or foot, view the city in a way not dreamed of at its eighteenth-century beginnings. Feather Air of Savannah provides hot air balloon rides according to riders' specifications.

Savannah Convention and Visitor's Bureau
800-444-CHARM (2427) / www.sacvb.com

Savannah Riverfront Association
912-234-0295

The Times on Bay
Bay Street (across from City Hall) / 912-232-5116

Old Pink House
23 Abercorn Street / 912-232-4286

Mrs. Wilke's Boarding House
107 West Jones Street / 912-232-5997

Hannah's East at the Pirate's House
20 East Broad Street / 912-233-2225

Bear Foot Sports
912-233-7764

Midnight in the Garden of Good and Evil Book Tour
912-233-3867

Carriage Tours of Savannah
912-232-6404

Southern Images Gallery
132 East Oglethorpe Street / 912-234-6449

Telfair Museum of Art
121 Barnard Street / 912-232-1177

Savannah Shadows Ghost Tour
912-233-0119

Haunting Tours
912-234-9255

Old Savannah Tours
912-234-8128

Feather Air of Savannah
912-858-2529

If you are looking for a preview near Savannah of the natural pleasures that await you on the coastal islands, Spartina Trails offer
various ways to explore Georgia's barrier islands. Aboard the company's boat, couples can eavesdrop on the underwater conversa-

tions of bottle-nosed dolphins and other sea creatures using hydrophones, be led on guided bird watching hikes along the seashore, or fish using a seine net.

Perhaps the most romantic souvenir you can take home from your time in Savannah is one of the handmade Pawley's Island rope hammocks brought direct from the South Carolina Low Country by The Hammock Company. You'll find them among the many regional crafts and local art at the famous City Market on Ellis Square in downtown Savannah.

Spartina Trails
912-234-4621

The Hammock Company
912-232-6655

City Market
912-232-4903

While in the Hostess City of the South, consider staying in one of the city's many small hotels or bed and breakfast inns. The city abounds with excellent accommodations romantically tucked away in graciously restored old homes and commercial buildings. There is something for every taste and budget and a complete list is available through the Convention and Visitor's Bureau.

The Ballastone Inn was once a grand Victorian house which slipped into service as a bordello and then into disuse, before being grandly restored. A favorite among romantics is the suite called Scarlett's Retreat with its fireplace, canopied English bed, and beautifully shuttered windows which reveal an allee of great old oaks.

The Ballastone Inn
14 E. Oglethorpe Avenue / Savannah / 800-822-4553

The 1896 Foley House Inn overlooks Chippewa Square where Tom Hanks, as Forrest Gump, sat philosophizing with his box of chocolates. Many of the rooms have fireplaces, four-poster beds, and small balconies.

Foley House Inn
14 West Hull Street / Savannah / 800-647-3708

THE BARRIER ISLANDS

After all the city pleasures and formal elegance of Old Savannah, its time to head to for the barefoot beaches of the barrier islands.

TYBEE ISLAND

The North Beach Grill is one of Tybee's favorite laid-back romantic spots. It retains the relaxed charm of a seafood shack and serves authentic Southern and Carribean favorites both inside and beachside. It is located on the northern end of the island directly across from the Tybee Lighthouse and Museum, an impressive romantic sight day or night. A lighthouse on Tybee Island has guided wary ships safely to port since 1736. Countless romances has been started or rekindled there, no doubt. The present day lighthouse is a beautiful setting perfect for a memorable photo. The Tybee Island Lighthouse and Museum is open year-round, except for major holidays. The owners of the North Beach Grill have also recently opened a more elegant counterpart, George's, perfect for a romantic dinner before a long walk on the beach.

North Beach Grill (next to the lighthouse)
912-786-9003

Tybee Island Lighthouse and Museum
912-786-5801 / www.Sonline.com/Tybee.light

 **George's**
Highway 80 (past the Lazaretto Creek Bridge) / 706-786-9730

OSSABAW ISLAND

Ossabaw Island is Georgia's first Heritage Preserve, the strongest level of environmental protection the state offers. Thus, the 26,000-acre barrier island twenty miles south of Savannah exists today in primordial splendor much the way it did millennia ago. The island is home to 200 archaeological sites and countless dolphins, osprey, herons, Abyssinian donkeys, wild boars, and endangered wood storks and loggerhead sea turtles. Through the Ossabaw Project, established in 1961 by Sandy West, the island has hosted an artist's colony which has attracted the likes of composers Aaron Copeland and Samuel Barber, novelists Ralph Ellison and Annie Dillard, and sculptor Harry Bertoria, among many others of note. Ossabaw Island is perfect for a very private, very simple getaway for either a daytrip or two or more nights of camping for small groups (groups are necessary as boat transportation must be specifically arranged for each party). While there you and your special someone can find time to yourselves to see the untouched maritime forest with its tidal creeks meandering through salt marshes, and the Grand Oak Alee dating from the islands ownership by Mary Bosomworth, General James Oglethorpe's interpreter.

Ossabaw Island Foundation
912-233-5104 / www.ossabawisland.org

BLACKBEARD ISLAND

While not especially hospitable to visitors, this exposed little island has a romantic history nonetheless. It is, in fact, named after Edward Teach, the high-seas pirate infamous as Blackbeard.

One of the many legends surrounding Teach was that he wore slow-burning, smoldering pieces of rope in his dark, overgrown beard to increase his fearsome appearance.

Formed into unusual shapes sometimes mimicking the curved forms of a ship's hull by the persistent pressure of the strong island winds, the gnarled knees and boughs of the island's countless live oaks were highly sought-after for shipbuilding. Wood for the frigate U.S.S. Constitution came from this dense old-growth forest and was nicknamed "Old Ironsides" after enemy cannonballs were said to have literally bounced off her hull in an engagement with the *H.M.S. Guerriere* in the War of 1812.

SAPELO ISLAND

Sapelo Island is the fourth largest of the barrier islands and is made up of a salt marsh maritime forest, beach and dune areas, and historic communities made famous in the pages of the book *Sapelo's People* by William McFeely. In addition to its rich biodiversity and cultural history, the romantic ruins of the Chocolate Plantation are located here, fronting the Mud River on the northwest shore of Sapelo.

Perhaps the best way to enjoy the romance of unspoiled culture and natural environment of Sapelo Island is to stay at The Weekender, a quaint campus of lodgings owned and operated by the permanent residents of the island. Located in Hog Hammock Community, a small colony of less than 100 permanent residents, The Weekender offers guests a choice of room or apartment rentals. The 147-passenger vessel *Annemarie* offers the only visitor access to the island, and its leisurely trip from the mainland affords the opportunity to view gamboling bottle-nosed dolphins in the tidal creeks and marshes. Meals are not provided in The Weekender but locals open their kitchens to visitors for one or two meals per day. This informal family-style dining gives visitors the opportunity to sample excellent soul food, red rice, steamed oysters, and fish fried fresh from the seine nets of Sapelo. Residents might also provide a tour of the Indian shell ring for a small fee. Visitors might want to take snacks and drinks in a cooler, although there is one general store on the island which sells essentials. Alcohol is not available for sale on the island. Bicycles are available for rental. It is possible to fly private planes onto the island's small airstrip, where Charles Lindbergh once landed.

The Weekender
912-485-2277 / www.gacoast.com/navigator/weekender.html

Perhaps the most romantic spot on the island is the site of the 1820 Sapelo Lighthouse which guided countless ships into the bustling nineteenth-century port of Darien. (The lighthouse was rebuilt in 1905 following a severe hurricane a few years previous.)

Sapelo Island National Estuarine Research Reserve offers guided tours focusing on the ecology and history of the barrier island. Guides discuss the salt marsh ecosystems, dunes, and maritime climax forests, as well as the historical visits to the islands by such notables as U.S. presidents Coolidge and Hoover, as well as aviator Charles Lindbergh. The reserve sponsors seasonal education programs.

Sapelo Island National Estuarine Research Reserve
912-485-2251

SEA ISLAND

Located across a short causeway from St. Simons Island or about an hour from Savannah lies Sea Island and The Cloister. This five-star hotel, a moss-draped marvel of 1920s Spanish-style romance, is frequently ranked among the world's great resorts and includes five miles of private beach, championship tennis and golf, lush gardens, spa, and historic sites, in addition to its incredible natural beauty. In addition to the Mobil Five-Star hotel, some of the private residences that make up the Cottage Colony are available for seasonal rental. Of the many romantic things to see and do on this small island, perhaps the most endearing is the annual Summer's End Dance Romance. The five-day dance clinic is part ballroom instruction, part end-of-summer party. Nationally and internationally renowned dance instructors show everyone from novices to experienced dancers everything from the waltz, fox trots, tangos, shag, and swing steps. As many as twelve complimentary classes are offered each day for every skill level.

Every August, the African American culture of the Georgia barrier island is celebrated through the Sea Island Festival in Neptune Park on St. Simons Island. This rich tapestry of basketmaking, music, dance, food, and cultural pride is not to be missed.

The Cloister
800-732-4752

LITTLE ST. SIMONS ISLAND

Only thirty guests have overnight accommodations at any one time on this 10,000-acre island paradise. Thus, you and your special someone will feel as though the seven miles of secluded beaches, coastal wilderness with Spanish moss-draped, 300-year old live oaks, and the rustically elegant cottages and lodges are yours and yours alone. The island is the perfect place for birdwatching, fishing, crabbing, riding, boating, and beachcombing.

The owners of the island operate Little St. Simons Island's four guest houses, dating from the 1910s to the present, and accommodate guests with three gourmet meals a day. The innkeepers will help make arrangements for everything from massages to guided interpretive nature programs to canoeing and boating excursions along the salt marshes. An Orvis-endorsed guide operates a saltwater fly fishing school which can be arranged through the innkeepers. Every month the innkeepers organize barge dinners and full-moon beach picnics for their guests. If twenty-eight other guests on the island is too much of a hubbub for you and your loved one, the entire island is available for private rental for you alone, dockage for your yacht included.

The Lodge on Little St. Simon's Island
P.O. Box 21078 / 912-638-7472 or 888-SEE-LSSI
www.pactel.com.au/lssi

St. Simons Island

Along with Jekyll, St. Simons Island is among the most visited of the Golden Isles. Here the charm lies in the island's colonial history and burgeoning art colony. Fort Frederica was established here in 1736 as protection for Savannah against Spanish invasion. The island is also the site of the 1886 Christ Church, built on the site of a church founded by the Wesley brothers, by Reverend Anson G. P. Dodge, Jr., as a memorial to his wife, Ellen, who died during the couple's honeymoon trip. Long-time St. Simons resident and novelist Eugenia Price (1916–1996) retold this story and other bits of local lore in her two novel cycles: her "St. Simons Trilogy" and her "Savannah Quartet."

St. Simons is also home to the Sea Palms Golf and Tennis Resort which offers twenty-seven challenging holes surrounded by majestic oaks, lush palmetto groves, and beautiful ponds.

The St. Simons Transit Company operates a water taxi to Jekyll from the Pier Village area of St. Simons in mid-afternoon and returns in mid-evening. Enjoy the shopping, horseback riding, restaurants, and historic sites of Jekyll Island. Bikes are welcome or can be rented from the St. Simons Transit Company itself. The company allows offers the option of planning your own trip on Jekyll, St. Simons, and environs.

St. Simons Transit Company
912-638-5678 or 912-635-3152

For a more heart-pounding way to see the coastal waters and salt marshes of St. Simons Island, try an air boat ride with Water Sports. The boat departs from the Golden Isles Marina on St. Simons Island and skims along the surface of the water on a cushion of air. Reservations for the U.S. Coast Guard inspected and certified air boat are required. The company also rents jet skis and offers parasailing.

Water Sports
912-638-SAIL (7245)

The St. Simons Lighthouse and Museum of Coastal History is one of the leading romantic landmarks on the Golden Isles. The 1872 tower is 104-feet tall and is tailor-made for the perfect photo to begin or end your visit to St. Simons. The tower and a small museum are open to the public. Climb to the top of the lighthouse just in time for the perfect sunset.

St. Simons Lighthouse and Museum of Coastal History
912-636-4666

JEKYLL ISLAND

Jekyll Island was once the very private escape of some of America's most affluent families. When the Civil War ended the cotton plantation economy, the island was sold in shares to wealthy Northerners. Goulds, Astors, Rockefellers, Morgans, and Pulitzers purchased the island as their personal province and built the Jekyll Island Club, a dining and sporting club, and the surrounding "cottage" colony. Now listed on the National Register of Historic Places, the 240-acre club operates as a hotel and restaurant, with impressive golf and tennis facilities and tournament croquet. By law only one-third of the island can be developed, thus the rarefied, Victorian elegance of the club is a beautiful contrast to the pristine natural beauty of the interior of the island. Nearly twenty miles of biking and walking trails, overhung with moss-draped live oaks, meander throughout the island.

Winter is perhaps the most romantic time to be on any beach, and this is especially true of Jekyll Island. A moody sky hangs over the beach deserted by the summer crowds, and with the salty chill of the breeze a couple can walk forever. Jekyll Island is transformed into a Christmas wonderland for the two weeks preceding the holiday. An annual tree lighting ceremony in the older section of town, itself decked out in thousands of twinkling lights, ushers in a nostalgic holiday. Volunteers from the local garden club deck out the resort town in seasonal greenery. The Jekyll Island Museum, site of restored historic cottages, offers tours, Victorian games and dances, cooking classes, and hayrides, all perfect for two in love. Musical activities range from big band dances to caroling parties. Lovers will want to make sure not to miss the Mistletoe Cottage.

For a bit of campy fun, Picture This will take a photo portrait of you and your special someone in the vintage costume of your choice. Imagine yourselves as an Old West gunfighter and saloon girl, Civil War soldier and belle, or Roaring '20s gangster and flapper. The studio is located in a historic district of shops.

Jekyll Island Museum Center
912-635-2762

Jekyll Island Club
71 Riverview Drive / 912-635-2600

Picture This
17A Pier Road / 912-635-3932

Bill's Island Tours will take you up, up, and away in its two-seater to see St. Simons Island from the air. Take an island hopping tour at sundown for good times and good photos. For a quieter tour of the historic district, Victoria's Carriages can arrange a horse-drawn carriage tour of the charming area.

Bill's Tours
912-222-2448

Victoria's Carriages
912-635-9500

Take a photo safari to capture the playfulness and acrobatics of the isles' large dolphin population. St. Simons Transit Company offers dolphin-watching tours departing from several Golden Isle locations, including the Jekyll Wharf Marina, Golden Isles Marina, and Epworth by the Sea, from early summer to early fall. Captain Fendig also operates a water taxi to St. Simons Island from Jekyll. Taxis journey to the Pier Village area of St. Simons in mid-afternoon and return to Jekyll mid-evening. Enjoy the shopping, restaurants, and historic sites of St. Simons Island. Bikes are welcome or can be rented from the company itself.

St. Simons Transit Company
912-638-5678 or 912-635-3152

The Coast Encounters Nature Center on Jekyll Island operates several educational tours of the area's rich salt marsh and sea ecosystems by foot, boat, and pond kayak. After learning together take a paddleboat ride for two on the center's seventeen-acre pond.

The Coast Encounters Nature Center
912-635-9102

In addition to sandals and hiking shoes, be sure to pack dancing shoes. The Jekyll Island Big Band claims a repertoire of over 200 swing, pop, and ballroom favorites. The band has public dances one Saturday a month at various locations on the island, sometimes in the open air.

Jekyll Island Welcome Center
800-841-6586 or 912-635-3636

CUMBERLAND ISLAND

The most bio-diverse and historically important barrier island in Georgia—and probably the entire East Coast—is Cumberland Island. The National Park Service owns and immaculately maintains eighty-five percent of the island's 36,000 acres. It is the largest and southernmost of Georgia's barrier islands. Only 300 visitors are allowed on the island each day. A passenger ferry operates between St. Mary's on the mainland and Cumberland Island with twice-daily arrivals and departures. Visitor population and ferry schedules are strictly adhered to—if you miss the last departure of the ferry, you must charter a boat for the return trip at your own expense. Visitor transportation on the island is strictly by foot.

The greatest attraction of the island is . . . nothing. But despite the island's miles of deserted beaches and unlimited solitude there is plenty to interest visitors. You can visit the First African Baptist Church (established in 1893 and rebuilt in the 1930s), the site of John F. Kennedy Jr.'s and Carolyn Bessette's wedding in 1996.

Overnight accommodations on the island vary from the rustic to the elegant. In addition to several wilderness camp sites, Cumberland has one developed campground. At Sea Camp Beach tents can be nestled among the dense growth of palmetto palms under the gently arching arms of the island's live oaks. The sites have restrooms, cold showers, and drinking water. Reservations and a camping permit are strictly required and may be obtained up to a year in advance.

🗼 **Sea Camp Ranger Station**
912-882-4335

The Pink Cottage is the restored and renovated former carpenter's quarters at Plum Orchard. The cottage is a simple stucco house with a wood stove and tin roof, overlooking the lush salt marshes along Brickhill River. Accommodations are simple, but the kitchen is well-equipped with cookware and appliances.

highlight

Island Inn

Picture perfect behind its picket fence on Darien's Vernon Square is the Open Gates Bed and Breakfast Inn. The white frame house was built with Italianate details in 1876 on the square of this town now listed on the National Register of Historic Places. The area has been written about in Melissa Fay Greene's Praying for Sheetrock and Fanny Kemble's Journal of Residence on a Georgian Plantation in 1838–1839. The house is painted in lively shades of Savannah blue and Pompeiian red and furnished throughout with sleigh beds, family quilts, and antiques. Darien is located halfway between Savannah and St. Mary's, so it makes an ideal place to stay if you're headed in either direction.

Open Gates Bed and Breakfast Inn
Vernon Square / Darien
912-437-985

The Pink Cottage
305-663-802

The 1901 Greyfield Inn still remains in the Carnegie family. Operated as an inn since the 1960s, Greyfield offers beautiful grounds, gourmet picnics under its lawn's massive trees, and candlelight dinners as the sun is setting. The inn is furnished in dark, heavy, late nineteenth-century furniture, some of which is original to the house. John F. Kennedy Jr. and Carolyn Bessette stayed at the Greyfield after their wedding ceremony. A two-car ferry, the *Lucy R. Ferguson,* operates between Fernandina Beach, Florida, and the inn on the southern end of the island. *The Lucy R. Ferguson* shuttles island visitors to and from the island. Small planes may also land on the inn's grass strip by prior arrangement.

Greyfield Inn
904-261-6408

A midnight walk on the beach turns magical when you venture from the beach into the dark tide. At each step the island's species of phosphorescent algae lights up around your feet. Days are filled with beachcombing and viewing the feral horses that feed and play among the tumbling ruins of million-dollar mansions. Or you can view the 1989 mansion, Plum Orchard, which Lucy Carnegie built as a wedding present for her son, or Thomas and Lucy Carnegie's ruined Dungeness built on the foundations of General Nathaniel Greene's circa–1783 tabby house of the same name.

spotlight

BUILD YOUR DREAM HOUSE
IN A DAY

You can build your dream house, whether its a replica of Cinderella's castle or a country cottage made for two. Your labor of love will be gone with the next high tide, but you'll have the memories forever. Following are a few of the best tips and tools for sand castle building.

The strongest sand castles are carved rather than built. Start by firmly packing wet sand into a block slightly larger than the structure you envision. (Natural salts in the sand will help it to stick together. Think of it as a block of very soft stone to be carved.) Your dream house should be sculpted from this firm block, rather than built with loose piles of dry sand. Begin carving away unwanted shapes from the top and work down to the foundation. Shave off thin layers to prevent crumbling and splitting. Details like spires and minarets can be "cast" in damp sand (using one's hands or a sand pail as a mold) and added back onto the structure later.

The smaller the roof in relation to the size of the walls, the stronger the structure is likely to be.

Don't forget landscaping. Moats, driveways, and fences add a lot of character. Trees can be created by slowing drizzling very wet sand through one's fingers.

spotlight

BUILD YOUR DREAM HOUSE IN A DAY

Tools can be fashioned from common objects, even from litter found on the beach. Flatten a soda can for use as a trowel or use a plastic water bottle with the bottom removed as a scoop. A hair comb can be dragged along flat surfaces to add texture, and a popsicle stick can be used to pierce small windows and doors into finished walls.

spotlight

THE SWEETHEART OF MANKIND

If you spend much time in the city, you are sure to see the lovely bronze statute of the Waving Girl, her dog at her side, on River Street in Savannah. The statue is dedicated to Florence Martus (1869–1943), known locally as "the sweetheart of mankind," and her story is as tragic as it is romantic.

She lived with and assisted her brother, the keeper of the Savannah light, located on Elba Island, about 7½ miles from the port of Savannah. Sometime in the early 1890s Florence bade farewell to her fiancé as he departed on a long sea journey. She made him the promise to greet every ship as it passed Elba Island so that she might be the first to welcome him upon his return. As the day of her beloved's return approached she kept her promise, running from the lightkeeper's house to wave her white apron at vessels approaching by day, and waving a lantern to ships passing at night. Countless waves were returned from onboard those ships, however none were ever those of her sea-faring fiancé. But as each ship passed by going down the river, her expression of stoic expectance never changed. Perhaps the next ship, or maybe the one after . . . Nearly a half-century passed and the port changed dramatically, ships bearing cargos of Low Country produce and Sea Island cotton increased manyfold, a world war began and ended, the Great Depression gripped the nation, but one thing remained constant—Savannah's waving girl, long since a woman, continued her lonely vigil on Elba Island. Her lookout ended in 1931 only because she was forced to move from Elba with her brother upon his retirement as lightkeeper. (He retired at age seventy, having held the position since 1887.) The bronze memorial now on Savannah's riverfront, sculpted by Felix De Weldon, was dedicated to her memory in 1971. On one side of the base of the statue, the following words are inscribed:

spotlight

THE SWEETHEART OF MANKIND

> *Her immortality stems from her*
> *friendly greeting to passing ships,*
> *a welcome to strangers entering the*
> *port and a farewell to wave them*
> *safely onward.*

Wining,
Dining,
and
Dancing

Kissing is like drinking salted water: you drink and your thirst increases.
—*Chinese proverb*

What romantic evening would be complete without the essential ingredients of wining, dancing, and dining? Whether your idea of restaurant romance is fine dining or an old-fashioned soda fountain, a civilized cocktail or a cold mug of suds, ballroom dancing or line dancing, Georgia has something for every taste.

There are so many great restaurants to choose from that it is impossible to set aside just a few in a book like this. Where it matches geographically throughout the book I have listed a few local favorites. Otherwise, take advantage of the local publications to discover a new place, or try a new cuisine. Whether your are looking to spend a lot of money with violins by your table or want to discover a new authentic, family-style Italian restaurant with a standard-issue red-checkered tablecloth and the flicker of a candle in a Chianti bottle, remember that you can make any experience a romantic one.

What follows is a guide to some of the unique experiences I've discovered, not just your typical restaurants.

TABLE FOR TWO

The 1848 House, in Marietta, serves contemporary Southern food in an elegant white-columned home. The restaurant is located on thirteen acres in the Bushy Park Plantation and is also known for its Jazz Brunch served every Sunday. Specialties include she-crab soup, rock shrimp cakes, and seasonal game. The Sweet Georgia Brown, a dark chocolate sponge cake with peanut butter ganache, is a favorite dessert. The 1848 House has been awarded Four Diamonds from AAA and Wine Spectator's Award of Excellence and has been featured in *Victoria* and *Food and Wine* magazines. The restaurant is listed on the National Register of Historic Places. After dinner, enjoy a play at the Theatre in the Square, named by *Southern Living* magazine as one of the South's most charming performance spaces.

The 1848 House
380 South Cobb Drive / Marietta / 770-428-1848
www.1848House.com

Theatre in the Square
11 Whitlock Avenue / Marietta / 770-422-8369

Jean Louise, in Savannah, is highly recommended by Savannahians as the city's most romantic restaurant. Named after chef John Jawback's daughter, the restaurant places as much emphasis on service and atmosphere as it does the freshness and presentation of its cuisine.

Jean Louise
321 Jefferson Street / Savannah / 912-234-3211

17Hundred90 Inn Restaurant and Lounge, located on the corner of East President and Lincoln streets in Savannah, is said to be haunted by a lover's ghost. Part of the complex of three buildings that make up the inn and restaurant is said to be built on foundations of older buildings dating to 1790. But it is the area now serving as garden seating and kitchen, constructed for prominent

Savannah merchant Steele White and his wife Anna in 1820, that has a ghostly romantic history. Local legend has it that White's new bride flung herself from the third-floor balcony over the brick-floored courtyard as the sails of her husband's ship dropped below the horizon of the Savannah River. Ghostly sightings and unexplained sounds are said to be frequent. Even without the dramatic story, the inn and restaurant are one of the city's most romantic restaurants. Reservations are strongly recommended.

17Hundred90 Inn Restaurant and Lounge
307 East President Street / Savannah
912-236-7122 or 800-487-1790

Enjoy a candlelight dinner as you cruise down the beautiful Savannah River on the *Savannah River Queen* or *Georgia Queen* paddleboats. The two-hour cruises depart from River Street behind City Hall in downtown Savannah and float you gently past landmarks of the city's founding, its cotton boom times, and the statue of Savannah's famous "Waving Girl" (see below). If you'd rather eat ashore, consider taking a moonlight cruise during which you can enjoy music and dancing. Reservations are required. If you want to surprise your date, call ahead and add a special occasion package to your river ride—champagne and flowers will be brought to your table.

River Street Riverboat Company
800-786-6404 / www.savannah-riverboat.com

Another Thyme Cafe is housed in the 1895 former Allen Pharmacy on the historic Washington main square. The dramatic space is highlighted with floor to ceiling windows, heart pine floors, and original brass schoolhouse lamps and converted brass chandeliers. The food is simple, but thoughtfully prepared.

Another Thyme Cafe
5 East Public Square / Washington / 706-678-1672

The Beehive Diner is as known for its imaginative, offbeat decor as it is for its basic, stick-to-your-ribs food. Sundaes, with two spoons, are a specialty.

The Beehive Diner
1090 Alpharetta Street / Roswell / 770-594-8765

The movie *Fried Green Tomatoes,* based on Fannie Flagg's novel *Fried Green Tomatoes at the Whistle Stop Cafe,* takes place in Whistle Stop, Alabama. The film was actually shot in Juliette, Georgia, a real-life town on the Ocmulgee River as close in spirit to the fictive Alabama town as can be found today. While you won't find the soul-searching Evelyn Couch, eighty-three-year-old Ninny Threadgoode, or the rebellious Idgie at the cafe, you will find the lightly battered Southern delicacy on the menu. The movie set is now home to various antique and craft stores and cafe owner Jerie Williams can fill a morning with her stories of the filming. Find the restaurant eight miles east of I-75 at Exit 61 in eastern Monroe County near the county seat of Forsyth. Try to arrange your travel back in time to coincide with the local Forsythia Festival, held annually as the vibrant yellow flowers come into bloom the second weekend in April; and include a visit to the twenty original buildings of the 1847 Jarrell Plantation.

Whistle Stop Cafe
Exit 61, U.S. I-75 / Juliette / 912-994-3670

Forsythia Festival
Juliette / 912-994-9239

Jarrell Plantation
711 Jarrell Plantation Road / Juliette / 912-986-5172

The Yesterday Cafe is famous for its sundaes, perfect for sharing. Housed in a renovated turn-of-the-century drugstore, the restaurant is also famous for its blueberry pancakes and buttermilk biscuits, as well as its country-fried steak with mashed potatoes.

The Yesterday Cafe
120 Fairplay Street / Rutledge / 706-557-9337

Dr. Hatchett's Drug Store Museum & Soda Fountain serves up milk shakes, blue plate specials, frozen fruit salad, flavored Cokes, and Coke served with peanuts. Located on the square in Lumpkin, the soda fountain is convenient to Browse-A-Bout Antiques, reportedly the source for some of Atlanta's most chi chi antique stores, and within easy driving distance of the 1850s living history village of Westville.

Dr. Hatchett's Drug Store Museum & Soda Fountain
Main Street / Lumpkin / 912-838-6924

Browse-A-Bout Antiques
Lumpkin / 912-838-6793

The Blue Willow Inn, nestled in Social Circle, offers intimate dining in a restored antebellum Greek Revival mansion. The menu is quintessentially Southern, and there is a dessert for every taste. It is just like the Sunday meal at Grandma's. Similarly, Dillard House offers resort lodging in elegant suites or cozy cottages in addition to its famous family-style restaurant. Dillard House is convenient to all the simple pleasures the Blue Ridge Mountains of north Georgia have to offer—waterfall hikes, antiquing, whitewater adventuring on the Chattooga River, or matching wills with large-mouth bass. Like the Dillard family, which has lived in the area since the Revolutionary War, you and your special someone can call the mountains home.

The Blue Willow Inn
294 North Cherokee Road / Social Circle / 770-464-2131

Dillard House
Highway 441 / Dillard / 800-541-0671 / www.dillardhouse.com

COOKING SCHOOLS

Cooking classes can be as romantic as they are practical. Sharing a favorite food, learning something new, getting a little messy—it's a perfect way to share time together. Demonstration classes are a fine way to learn, but participation classes are really where the action is.

Besides being one of Atlanta's most romantic eateries, the Food Studio also offers single-session cooking classes around special holidays and seasonal themes. Culinary Institute of America-trained chef Chris Brandt offers morning-long classes monthly, usually on the last Saturday. Lunch with wine is provided.

The Food Studio
887 W. Marietta Street, NW, Studio K-102 / Atlanta
404-815-6677

Cuisine Arts has offered demonstration and participation classes for more than a decade. Located in Big Canoe, the classes are offered by former Atlanta caterer Jan Shackleford. The eclectic themes range from a Cuban dinner to cheeses from around the world to a spring supper. The single session, three-and-one-half hour classes are offered once a month, usually on the last Thursday.

Cuisine Arts
9141 Shetland Trace / Big Canoe / 706-268-3776
jan_shackelford@ipipe.com

The Rolling Pin Cooking School offers two-hour, single-session classes taught by caterers and chefs from the Athens area. Marti Schimmel, owner of Gourmet to Go Catering company, teaches many of the classes which range from sushi-making, food and wine pairings, holiday baking, and soups and sauces.

Rolling Pin Kitchen Emporium
Beechwood Shopping Center / 196 Alps Road / Athens
706-354-8080

Anita LaRaia's Wine School has been offering instruction in wine styles, grape varieties, tasting and wine and food pairing for over twenty years. LaRaia learned about wine during an apprenticeship in London and has ten years' experience in wine retailing and importing. Classes are taught with lectures and wine tastings in six weekly, one-hour sessions. Classes are usually taught at the Wyndham Garden Hotel in the Buckhead neighborhood of Atlanta.

Anita LaRaia's Wine School
Wyndham Garden Hotel / 3340 Peachtree Road, NE / Atlanta
770-901-9433 / anitalaraia@mindspring.com

WINERIES

North Georgia offers a variety of vineyards and wineries for both afficionados and the casually interested. Tours and tasting rooms can be a fun and informative way to spend an afternoon, and the beautiful mountain scenery, particularly in the fall, only adds to the experience.

The largest winery in the state, Château Élan, in Braselton, is also known for its resort, restaurant, spa, golf course, and equestrian center. You might choose to take the hour-long vineyard tour and spend a few moments in the tasting room, or you might opt to spend a three-day weekend enjoying all there is to do. Personalized wine labels are available for special occasions. The winery is located off exit 48 of I-85.

Château Élan
100 Tour de France / Braselton / 800-233-WINE (9463)
www.chateauelan.com / chateau@chateauelan.com

With several tasting rooms across north Georgia, the Habersham Winery wines are actually made at its Baldwin County facility. The first bottle was corked in 1983 and production has since risen to 10,000 cases a year. Tours are available upon request, and free and moderately priced tastings are given daily.

Habersham Winery
Baldwin / 706-778-9463

The Chestnut Mountain Winery is a very small, very charming wine making operation in Braselton. The winery produces a total of 2,500 cases annually, the best known of which is their Cabernet Sauvignon. In addition to hosting festivals in April and October, the owners will take visitors on a brief tour of the vineyard upon request. Chestnut Mountain also has a tasting counter and retail operation.

Chestnut Mountain Winery
Braselton / 770-867-6914

BARS

Buckhead Fine Wine Bar & Cafe is known for its first-rate selection of French reds by the taste, glass, or bottle. A meal can be made of its sophisticated appetizers, or the house specialties—truffled duck terrine, chicken mousse, and beef tenderloin medallions, among them—can be ordered from the full menu. The beautiful decor of this modern bistro, especially its elegant glassware, add a special note to the evening.

Buckhead Fine Wine Bar & Cafe
1155 Mount Vernon Highway
Atlanta / 770-390-0440

The ultimate nightcap, the Four Seasons Sampler, is available in the lounge of Atlanta's Four Seasons Hotel. Four miniature cocktails of your choosing are served on a silver tray. Think of it as the grown-up version of sampling the flavors at Baskin-Robbins. This beautiful luxury hotel is convenient to midtown Atlanta's many theaters, museums, and restaurants.

The Four Seasons
75 Fourteenth Street / Atlanta
404-881-9898

The Martini Club was the first in Atlanta to celebrate the rediscovery of your

found at Happy Herman's (404-321-3012) at 2299 Cheshire Bridge Road. Alon's Bakery is also known for its fine semolina bread at its locations at 1394 N. Highland (404-872-6000) or at the Georgian Terrace (404-724-0444) at 659 Peachtree Street. The knowledgeable staff at Ansley Wine Merchants (404-876-6790) will recommend the perfect red or white at their location at the Ansley Square Mall at 1544 Piedmont Road. Smoak's Bakery (706-733-5931) is the bakery in Augusta. Visit their shop at 2058 Walton Way before heading to choose from the fine selection at Wine World (706-733-5931), just over the bridge in North Augusta at 106 Georgia Avenue. Then head for either of the most scenic picnic spots in Augusta, the relaxed Pendleton-King Park or the always active Augusta Riverwalk (706-821-175).

grandparents' favorite cocktail. They offer 101 different types of martinis in a jazz-filled Deco lounge. Soft music, softer lights, and the softest gin make Goldfinger one of Atlanta's favorite high-style nightclubs. The bar's namesake is the arch enemy of that icon of all things martini, James "Shaken, Not Stirred" Bond.

The Martini Club
1140 Crescent Avenue / Atlanta / 404-873-0794

Goldfinger
3081 East Shadowlawn Avenue / Atlanta / 404-627-8464

JAZZ CLUBS

Blind Willie's, named after Blind Willie McTell, Georgia's most famous and authentic bluesman, is a down-and-dirty blues club in Atlanta which features some of the best national blues musicians. This Virginia Highlands' neighborhood favorite also serves excellent Cajun food and ice-cold beer.

Blind Willie's
828 North Highland Avenue / Atlanta / 404-873-BLUE (2583)

Two Savannah clubs—as different as night and day—share all the requisites for a hot jazz spot: torch songs and smoky ambience. Devin Michael's, on the corner of West Broughton and Whitaker, looks like a college kid's dive, but the cutting-edge jazz and touring acts are first-rate. Hannah's East, upstairs at the Pirate's House, has a sultry, nostalgic decor, with some of the best jazz to be heard anywhere. Emma "The Lady with 6,000 Songs" Kelly, immortalized in John Berendt's bestseller *Midnight in the Garden of Good and Evil* performs there for enthusiastic audiences from her immense repertoire of standards, show tunes, and torch songs.

Devin Michael's
30 West Broughton Street / Savannah / 912-232-6887

Hannah's East at the Pirate's House
20 East Broad Street / Savannah / 912-233-2225

DIVES

It's not too hard to find a favorite dive and many will rank right up there in the *un*-romantic Hall of Fame. But, a good dive can be very romantic depending on your perspective and willingness to look past decor in exchange for a memorable experience, perhaps cheap drinks and a quick game of pool while listening to a local honky tonk band. They don't call it "local color" for nothing.

Dottie's may look a little seedy on the outside, but the crowd inside is always warm and welcoming. Dottie's has live music— from punk to country to alternative—almost every night, and its postage stamp-sized dance floor is always jam-packed on weekends. Periodically, some of the best local musicians stage "Battles of the Bands" in which two bands pay homage to their arena rock favorites in winner-takes-all cover contests. Contests included Rolling Stones vs. The Who, Bauhaus vs. Joy Division, and two-mock AC/DC bands trying to win bragging rights.

Dottie's
307 Memorial Drive, SE / Atlanta / 404-523-3444

On the outskirts of the increasingly gentrified Poncey Highland neighborhood of Atlanta is a little strip of shops and restaurants lit by Art Deco-inspired neon designs. At the center of this eclectic group of businesses is the Righteous Room, the perfect joint to dive into after a bite at the Majestic Food Shop greasy spoon or an art house flick at the Lefont Plaza Theater. Locals of every description—Big Chill Boomers, Gen-X hipsters, and everyone in between—come for the Righteous Room's feel of a Greenwich Village coffee house and its arm-long list of beers. It is the eclectic jukebox—perhaps the best in the city—that is this dive's claim to fame.

The Righteous Room
1051 Ponce de Leon Avenue / Atlanta / 404-874-0939

Majestic Food Shop
1031 Ponce de Leon Avenue / Atlanta / 404-875-0276

Lefont Plaza Theater
1049 Ponce de Leon Avenue / Atlanta / 404-873-1939

DANCING

The Imperial Fez restaurant is straight out of Casablanca. Diners can recline on floor cushions and Berber tribe-woven rugs worthy of a sultan while they dine on a feast of Moroccan finger food and extraordinary tajines and couscous. Accomplished belly dancers rock the Casbah with nightly floor shows. If you enjoy the show, you might consider taking private lessons from one of the several dancers who take students on the side.

The Imperial Fez
2285 Peachtree Road / Atlanta / 404-827-0040
www.mindspring.com/~rafih

At its twice monthly dances, the Atlanta Cajun Dance Association welcomes newcomers and experienced Cajun dancers alike to celebrate the music and food of this unique Louisiana culture. Lessons are given in the basics of the Cajun two-step and the zydeco hop before the dance hall fills up. But the point is not to look like Fred and Ginger, it's to listen to the music, enjoy a cold beer with the spicy food, and dance, dance, dance. ACDA holds dances with Zydeco bands on the second and fourth Saturday of every month at the Knights of Columbus Post 660.

Atlanta Cajun Dance Association
770-451-6611

Knights of Columbus Post 660
2620 Buford Highway, NE / Atlanta / 404-636-9237

The Boot Scoot Boogie Bash held annually at the Savannah Rapids Pavilion in August is an evening of line dancing, dinner, and a silent auction. Everyone from greenhorns to expert line dancers can join in the hootenanny. You'll get rosy cheeks from this sexy two-step and a warm glow knowing that you and your partner have helped the American Red Cross.

American Red Cross/Augusta Chapter
706-724-8481

The Athens Folk Music and Dance Society holds a friendly and fun contra dance the third Saturday of each month in the ballroom of Memorial Hall on the University of Georgia campus. The monthly dances feature a mix of traditional American contras, circles, waltzes, and sometimes squares (the official state folk dance of Georgia). All are performed to live music from the society's members or visiting musicians. Beginner's lessons precede the start of the dance. The society holds "Hoots," or parties with food, music, and dancing, the second Monday of each month at various places around the Athens area to which all newcomers are welcome. This group of folk dance afficionados is as serious about fun as they are about music preservation, and will provide a newsletter and monthly dance schedule upon request.

🎵 **The Athens Folk Music and Dance Society**
P.O. Box 346 / Athens / www.negia.net/~laurenzo/

Atlanta's liveliest guys and dolls can be found jitterbugging at Swingers in Atlanta. This juke joint offers free swing lessons every night at 10 P.M. Atlanta's 37,000 square foot Masquerade also offers free lessons with DJ Spike every Sunday night at its location in the once-abandoned 1890 Excelsior Mill. Capture the fun of your swingin' evening in a picture in the photo booth in Purgatory. (The Masquerade is a complex of three bars in one—Heaven, Hell, and Purgatory—with stone and brick walls, iron chandeliers, and languishing industrial equipment. The 4,000-person capacity, one-acre Masquerade Music Park amphitheater is attached.) Both Swingers and The Masquerade get jumping after the lessons end.

🎵 **Swingers**
3449 Peachtree Road / Atlanta / 404-816-9931

🎵 **Masquerade**
695 North Avenue / Atlanta / 404-577-2002
www.masq.com/pages/mainpage.html
masq@masq.com

Cha-cha-cha! Sambuca Jazz Café has plenty of swing. Its large, romantically lit dance floor hosts Atlanta's best swing bands. Located in Atlanta's vibrant nightlife capital of Buckhead, there are—according to the *Atlanta Journal Constitution*—more than one hundred bars within the two-and-one-half block radius of the intersection of Peachtree Road and West Paces Ferry Road.

🎵 **Sambuca Jazz Café**
3102 Piedmont Road / Atlanta / 404-237-5299

The truly romantic dance is the tango, and the truly authentic form is the Argentine tango. The cheek-to-cheek dance was created by the Uruguayan Gerardo Matos Rodriguez on the shore of the Rio de la Plata in Buenos Aires and Montevideo, hence the name rioplatense, and it is the most renowned of all tangos. Milongas, or dance parties, are held two Sundays a month in various locations around Atlanta.

Manuel or Ronda Patino
Atlanta / 404-377-5822 / www.tango-rio.com/index.htm

Ooh la-la!

Who, being loved, is poor?—Oscar Wilde

Love—one of the best things in life—is free. But celebrating it can sometimes set you back. And although the greatest gift one can give is love, it's a gift one will want to see returned. Here are a few ideas perfect for an anniversary, a birthday, or maybe just an everyday splurge.

INDULGENCE IN ATLANTA

Tiffany & Company is famous throughout the world for its gorgeous collection of everything gold and glittery. The selection seems endless: from the sublime (the store's signature six-prong setting—the "Tiffany setting" for platinum and diamond engagement rings) to the ridiculous (the sterling telephone dialer that Holly Golightly perused in the 1961 film version of Truman Capote's *Breakfast at Tiffany's*). All purchases are wrapped in the store's signature robin's egg blue boxes tied prettily with white satin ribbon. Phipps Plaza offers some of the Southeast's best shopping. Its flagship department store, Saks Fifth Avenue, is surrounded by a label-hoarder's dream of Gucci, Prada, Jil Sander, and Gianni Versace boutiques, among many others. If the boutique's prices are out of your reach, grab a pastry and coffee at Il Centro Caffee or Karl Bissinger's French Confections at Phipps and enjoy a window-shopping breakfast at Tiffany's a la Holly.

If your day of haute shopping leaves you feeling like you've run the Peachtree Marathon, reinvigorate at the afternoon tea at the Ritz Carlton Buckhead's Lobby Lounge conveniently located next door to Phipps. High tea, consisting of a pot of tea of your choice and a generous plate of sweets and sandwiches is a real treat. To make the afternoon a little more special, sherry may be ordered from the bar.

Tiffany & Company
Phipps Plaza / 3500 Peachtree Road / Atlanta / 404-261-0074

Il Centro Café
Phipps Plaza / 3500 Peachtree Road / Atlanta / 404-364-9313

Karl Bissinger's French Confections
Phipps Plaza / 3500 Peachtree Road / Atlanta / 404-237-7161

Ritz Carlton Buckhead
3434 Peachtree Road / Atlanta / 800-241-3333 or 404-237-2700

SPAS

The Spa at Château Élan, located at the Braselton winery, offers a "Spa Getaway" package which includes spa basics (including steam, sauna, whirlpool, and use of fitness equipment, including use of a bike to tour the grounds), as well as a facial, pedicure, thalassotherapy underwater massage, Swedish massage, salt glow with Vichy shower, and make-up application for her or scalp treatment for him. The package includes meals at the winery's various restaurants and afternoon teas. End the day with a complimentary winery tour with tastings. Spa-goers can use the château's library and borrow from the video and compact disc collection for after-hours entertainment as a part of the package, or use the château élan's golf and tennis facilities for an extra charge.

The Spa at Château Élan
100 Tour de France / Braselton / 800-233-WINE (9463)
www.chateauelan.com / chateau@chateauelan.com

Joseph & Friends Salon and Day Spa is a full service day spa which can develop packages around a couple's needs.

Joseph & Friends Salon and Day Spa
1570 Holcomb Bridge Road, Suite 205 / Roswell / 770-993-0058

In the heart of downtown Atlanta's hotel district and its theaters, clubs, and restaurants is the Spa at Peachtree Center Athletic Center. The "Day Spa Experience" package begins with a morning fitness class of your choice followed by relaxation in the hot tub or steamroom. Pampering treatments begin with an Aveda brand Pre-Treatment Body Polish in preparation for a relaxing Moor Mudd Body Masque accompanied by a facial and aromatherapy scalp massage. Finally, a full hour of Swedish massage is completed with a manicure and pedicure. Get a healthy bite to eat after your treatment in the fifteenth-floor restaurant.

The Spa at Peachtree Center Athletic Center
227 Courtland Street / Atlanta
404-523-3833

The several metro-Atlanta locations of Spa Sydell all offer a variety of soothing, restorative treatments and a "His and

Hers Body Massage" which can be enjoyed separately or as part of a package of other indulgences. Call the flagship spa for a selection of services and spa treatments at all the various locations.

Spa Sydell
5064 Roswell Road, Suite A / Atlanta / 404-816-0048
www.spasydell.com

Key Lime Pie Salon and Wellness Spa, in the fun and funky Virginia Highlands neighborhood of Atlanta, specializes in aromatherapy facials and has a scented hydrotherapy tub. Clients are welcome to design their own packages. The spa is surrounded by a neighborhood of fun shops, trendy restaurants, and theaters. Reportedly past clients have included Natalie Merchant, the Indigo Girls, and Monica Seles.

Key Lime Pie Salon and Wellness Spa
806 North Highland Avenue / Atlanta / 404-873-6512

Natural Body Day Spa in Atlanta gives classes in several massage techniques from the relaxing to the invigorating. You are free to share your homework with your partner.

Natural Body Day Spa
1403 North Highland Avenue / Atlanta / 404-876-9642

BED & BREAKFAST INNS

Some of the best pampering awaits you off the beaten path. Following is a list of a few of the best bed and breakfast inns in the state.

The Shellmont Bed & Breakfast Inn is located in an 1891 National Registered mansion surrounded by the glittering skyscrapers of midtown Atlanta. The interior is a Victorian hodge-podge of intricately carved woodwork and hand-painted stenciling. The veranda looks out onto manicured lawns and gardens and a Victorian fishpond.

Shellmont Bed & Breakfast
821 Piedmont Avenue, NE / Atlanta / 404-872-9290

The simple 1913 Craftsman exterior of Atlanta's Gaslight Inn belies its poshly appointed interiors. The inn offers affordably elegant rooms and luxurious suites, all decorated by the city's well-known Pineapple House Interior Design. The house, with its walled garden and eleven fireplaces, is in the city's eclectic Virginia Highlands neighborhood. If you crave aloneness, the Ivy Cottage is a detached bungalow with a living room, full kitchen and laundry facilities behind the main house. Elaborate breakfasts are prepared by one of the proprietors, an expert chef profiled in *Bon Appetit*. The Gaslight Inn has been featured in *Better Homes and Gardens, Southern Homes,* and *Atlanta Homes and Lifestyles.*

The Gaslight Inn
1001 St. Charles Avenue, NE / Atlanta / 404-875-1001

Known as the Holberg Hotel in 1906, the two-story neoclassical house, The Veranda, now serves as a bed and breakfast. According to some sources, the one-time hotel was the home of many former Confederate soldiers and Margaret Mitchell interviewed many of them there for *Gone With the Wind.* Five-course dinners are served nightly. In addition to its kaleidoscope collection and player piano, the house is filled with antiques and curiosities of every sort, as befits an inn in a town with 140 sites—like the inn itself—on the National Register of Historic Places.

The Veranda
252 Seavy Street / Senoia / 770-599-3905

The quiet of Watkinsville's main street and the calm of the 1893
Queen Anne exterior of Ashford Manor give no clue to the riot of
color and lively design inside. One of the three owner/residents is
a former theater designer and rock music costumer and the whole
of the bed and breakfast has a suitably eclectic bent. Besides the
house, a cottage, gazebo, and swimming pool are situated in four
acres of landscaped gardens which terrace down to open woods
and a creek. The five guest rooms, two bedroom suite and two-
story "penthouse" suite with Jacuzzi are appointed with antiques
and artifacts from the charming owners' world travels. Several
shops and galleries are within easy walking distance, including
Ruggiere: A Gallery, a popular shop featuring work by local craft
and folk artists.

Ashford Manor
5 Harden Hill Road / Watkinsville / 706-769-2633

Ruggiere: A Gallery
12 Main Street / Watkinsville / 706-769-7247

I LOVE YOU

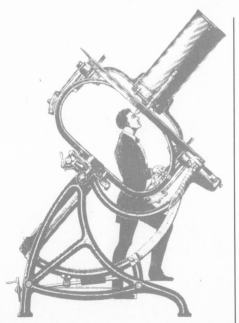

The
Unexpected

You call it madness, but I call it love.—Don Byas

When we think of romance we often think of can-
dlelit dinners, gifts of long-stemmed roses, and bottles of vintage
champagne. While those sentimental expressions are certainly
wonderful, there are other ways to say "I love you" that might suit
other tastes and moods. Following are ideas perfect for the offbeat, the secretly sappy, and those who love to dance—but to a
different drummer. These venues are the best of the best, but similar ones are waiting to be discovered in your own backyard.

FOR THOSE WHO SEEK THE UNIQUE

Take the plunge. Air Ventures in Rome offers tandem skydiving
training. After a forty-five minute class you and your little daredevil can take a heart-pounding jump from 13,500 feet near Air
Venture's base at the Floyd County airstrip. The jumps offer scenic
views of the foothills of the Appalachians.

 Air Ventures
Richard B. Russell Airfield / Rome / 706-234-3087

POETRY WITH SOUL

On the first Tuesday of every month, poetry readings and spoken
word performances are given at Café Diem in the funky Poncey-

Highland neighborhood of Atlanta. It's a chance to hear passion-
ate poets bare their souls—or read your own love poem—all for
the price of a cup of joe.

> **Café Diem**
> **642 North Highland Avenue / Atlanta / 404-607-7008**

GO PLAY IN THE DIRT

Art & Soul in Atlanta provides budding ceramicists unpainted,
unfired pottery which you and your loved one can paint and dec-
orate as you chose. How about his-and-hers coffee mugs painted
in such a way that when you both finish your second cup at the
office a thoughtful inscription is visible inside. The café fires your
creations for you in their own kiln and you can pick them up a
few days later. The studio is located in the Brookwood Shopping
Center behind the popular Houston's Restaurant, known for its
artichoke and spinach dip and huge salads and steaks, served on
its brick-paved patio. Similar studios are Wired & Fired: A Pottery
Playhouse in Athens and Midnight Star Pottery in Savannah.

> **Art & Soul: An Arts & Craft Café**
> **2140 Peachtree Road, NW / Atlanta / 404-352-1222**

> **Wired & Fired: A Pottery Playhouse**
> **120 East Clayton Street / Athens / 706-543-4006**

> **Midnight Star Pottery**
> **32 Barnard Street / Savannah / 912-236-3473**

GLOW-IN-THE-DARK ACTION

Brunswick Cedar Creek Lanes in Marietta features lights-out
Cosmic Bowling with glow-in-the-dark pins and balls after mid-

nights on weekends. A disc jockey spins all the retro-hits for the forty lanes of bowlers and the games go on til 4 A.M. U.S. Play is another trippy bowling experience with pins and balls that glow-in-the-dark, a fog machine, a disco ball and cheesy dance music.

Brunswick Cedar Creek Lanes
2749 Delk Road / Marietta / 770-988-8813

U.S. Play
775 Cobb Place Boulevard / Kennesaw / 770-427-7679

LOOKING FOR PEACE AND QUIET

The Cistercian monks at the Monastery of the Holy Spirit in Conyers train and sell beautiful bonsai to help fund their abbey. The bonsai is on sale at the brothers' conservatory in the isolated, austere beauty of the cloistered retreat. A large lake with ducks and swans always hungry for a hand-out makes for a lovely day.

Monastery of the Holy Spirit
2625 Hwy. 212, SW / Conyers / 770-483-8705 / www.ga.monks.org

HEADED TO PARADISE

Reverend Howard Finster's three-acre Paradise Garden has been described as a "pop-art Eden with a born-again twist." Beginning in 1961, this visionary artist has created a series of Biblical and cautionary tableaux in his Summerville garden made of found objects and his trademark images of Elvis and Hank Williams. No longer laboring in obscurity, his work is sought after by museums and collectors worldwide, and has graced the covers of R.E.M. and Talking Heads CDs. This realization of this artist's extraordinary vision can be found approximately twenty-one miles northeast of Rome in Chattooga County. You may want to stay overnight at the garden in the Paradise Suite. For true aficionados, go to the annual Howard Finster Festival, held annually the second Saturday in May at Dowdy Park in Summerville.

🌲 **Finster Folk Art**
Summerville / 706-857-2926

GO CLIMB A TREE

You can take your love to the top of the world when you spend an afternoon with Tree Climbers International. The Atlanta-based group supports and instructs in "technical tree climbing." With the use of simple equipment similar to rappeling ropes, even novices and the short-winded can scale a huge tree in a matter of minutes. It's a safe and simple way to bring out the child in anyone. The group maintains an active schedule of classes and planned outings.

🏚 **Tree Climbers International**
628 West College Avenue / Decatur / 404-377-9663
www.treeclimbing.com

BE A KID AGAIN

The Lunch Box Museum in Columbus has over 3,000 steel and plastic lunch boxes and 2,000 Thermoses that are sure to get a fun and nostalgic conversation going. Baby boomers are said to get almost misty-eyed as they see these prime pieces of childhood memorabilia—schoolyard renderings of *The Jetsons*, *Lost in Space*, and *The Lone Ranger*. If you take a picnic lunch—maybe a bologna sandwich with carrot sticks and a carton of chocolate milk—for gosh sakes, *don't* brown bag it.

🏚 **The Lunch Box Museum**
1236 Broadway (the second floor of 106-FM radio station)
Columbus / 800-445-4106

PARADISE BY THE DASHBOARD LIGHT

The antique car museum in tiny Cartersville, Old Car City USA, is called by automotive aficionados "Dream Town." Besides its stand-out collection of horseless carriages and vintage roadsters, there is also a display of antique toys. The highlight of the museum is what is claimed to be Elvis Presley's last car.

Old Car City USA
Highway 411 North / Cartersville / 770-382-6141

GIVE THE OUTDOORS AS A GIFT

Unusual and hard-to-find heritage (non-hybridized or species) roses perfect for building a Victorian rose garden together. Some roses were introduced in the sixteenth century and later Austin roses bear names such as Dapple Dawn, Shropshire Lass, and Immortal Juno. Find every romantic rose from teacups to damasks at the well-stocked nursery.

The Antique Rose Emporium
5565 Cavender Creek Road / Dahlonega / 706-864-5884

VINTAGE LOVE

Vintage clothing retailers are a good source for all the romantic attire designers just don't seem to make anymore. But if you are a budding Valentino or Theda Barra, Stephan's in Atlanta's hipper-than-thou Little Five Points neighborhood stocks dressing gowns, smoking jackets, nightgowns, and lingerie from the 1930s on. Folks have been known to travel from several states away to inspect Stephan's wares. But vintage clothing stores of all types (and prices) are in most cities. Find a good store near you and play dress-up with the one you love.

Stephan's
1160 Euclid Avenue / Atlanta / 404-688-4949

TELL THE WORLD YOU'RE IN LOVE

Maybe you have to spell it out for that special someone to really understand just how you feel and a billboard can say it all. Two companies in Atlanta arrange for billboard rentals throughout the state: Eller Media Company and Outdoor Systems Advertising. Just think of it as help for the hopeless romantic who is helplessly tongue-tied. Prices vary widely depending on size, location, and length of contract.

Eller Media Company
Atlanta / 404-875-0822

Outdoor Systems Advertising
Atlanta / 404-699-1499

LOOK TO THE HEAVENS

If you've promised all this and heaven too, now you can deliver. Why not have a plane fly overhead bearing behind it a banner emblazoned with your loving message. Even better if you make the arrangements while you and your honey are at a public event in a park or stadium. That way the whole world sees that you're in love, and the reaction that goes with it. The cost is surprisingly reasonable for a one-hour pass with a reasonably long message. Perhaps: Will you marry me? There are companies at small and large airports across the state who provide the service. In Atlanta, several companies work out of Peachtree-DeKalb Airport and serve a surprising large area surrounding the city, as far out as Athens, Gainesville, and Rome.

Barbara's Banners & Balloons
Atlanta / 770-228-0965

Index

Actor's Express Theater 16
Adairsville 43
AdVentures Aloft 61
Agatha's—A Taste of
  Mystery 16
Air Ventures 139
Alliance Theater 16
Alon's 10
Alon's Bakery 121
Alpharetta 66
Alpine Tubing 77
American Red
  Cross/Augusta Chapter
  125
Amicalola Falls 48, 73
Amicalola Falls State Park
  79
Amicalola River Rafting
  Outpost 78
Anita LaRaia's Wine School
  119
Anna Ruby Falls 74
Annie Hall 11
Another Thyme Café 116
Ansley Wine Merchants
  121
Antique Rose Emporium
  143
Appling 47
Art & Soul: An Arts and
  Crafts Café 140
Arts Experiment Station 18

Ashford Manor 136
Athens Folk Music and
  Dance Society 126
Athens 4, 16, 40, 42, 14,
  15, 119, 126, 140
Atlanta Opera 3
Atlanta Shakespeare Tavern
  17
Atlanta Symphony
  Orchestra 7
Atlanta 3, 4, 5, 6, 7, 8, 10,
  12, 13, 14, 15, 16, 17,
  18, 23, 41, 46, 55, 60,
  69, 70, 118, 119, 120,
  121, 122, 123, 124, 125,
  126, 132, 133, 134, 135,
  140, 144
Atlanta Ballet 5
Atlanta Botanical Gardens
  40
Atlanta Braves 61
Atlanta Bread Garden 120
Atlanta Cajun Dance
  Association 125
Atlanta Preservation Society
  23
Atlanta Symphony
  Orchestra 6
Augusta 4, 12, 23, 32, 47,
  67, 69, 121
Augusta Canal Authority
  32, 67, 69

Augusta Riverwalk 46, 121
Augusta Opera Association
  4
Augusta Riverboat Cruises
  44
Austell 45
Ballastone Inn 94
Ballethnic Dance Company
  5
Balloon Safaris
  International 61
Barbara's Banners and
  Balloons 144
Barnsley Gardens 43
Barry's Beach Service 101
Bear Foot Sports 93
Beehive Diner 116
Bendzunas Glass Gallery
  133
Big Chill 10
Big Canoe 118
Bill's Tours 102
Biplanes Over Atlanta 60
Blairesville 36, 54
Blakely 29
Blind Willie's 122
Blue Willow Inn 118
Braselton 62, 84, 120, 132
Brasstown Bald 54
Brasstown Bald Visitors
  Center 36
Breakfast at Tiffany's 9, 131

Bridges of Madison County 27
Broad River Outpost 78
Browse-A-Bout Antiques 117
Brunswick Cedar Creek Lanes 141
Buckhead Fine Wine Bar & Café 121
Bullock Hall 86
Burt's Farm 48
Butts Mill Farm 65
Café Diem 140
Calhoun 49
Callaway Gardens 37, 66
Canoe the Flint 69
Michael C. Carlos Museum of Art 12
Carnes' Nectar of the Wild 51
Carriage Tours of Savannah 93
Cartersville 68, 143
Cator Woolford Garden 40
Cave Springs Art Festival 19
Cave Springs 19
Center for Puppetry Arts 13
Chamblee 60
Charis Books 15
Chastain Park Amphitheater 6
Château Élan Golf Club 62, 84
Château Élan 62, 120
Chatsworth 35, 80
Chattahoochee Outdoor Nature Center 59
Chestnut Mountain Winery 120
Chief Vann House State Historical Site 35
City Market 94
Clarkesville 69, 82
Clayton 51
Clayton State University 6

Cloister 62, 63, 99
Cloudland Canyon State Park 36
Clyde Dunaway Bicycles 32
Coast Encounters Nature Center 104
Cohutta Lodge and Restaurant 80
Cold Sassy Tree 11
Columbus 23, 142
Comer 133
Conant Performing Arts Center 18
Conyers 141
Cool River 77
Coosa River Christmas Lighted Boat Parade 51
Covered Bridge Trail of Georgia 27
Crabapple 66
Cuisine Arts 118
Cumberland Island 104
Dahlonega 11, 66, 80, 143
Dalton 35
Daniellesville 78
Darien Chamber of Commerce 90
Darien 105
Davidson-Arabia Mountain Nature Preserve 54
Decatur 9, 12, 14, 15, 54, 142
Dene's General Store 51
DePalma's Italian Café 14
Devin Michael's 123
Dillard 33, 81, 118
Dillard House 33, 118
Dottie's 123
Double Q Farms 48
Dr. Hatchett's Drug Store Museum and Soda Fountain 117
Driving Miss Daisy 10, 39
Drop Squad 10
Dunwoody 59
E Shaver Fine Books 14

Eagle Adventure Company 65
Eddie Collins Island Bike Shop 101
1848 House 114
Einstein's 70
Elachee Nature Science Center 44
Eller Media Company 144
Emory University 12
Euharlee Creek Bridge 29
F.D.R. Riding Stables 65
Feather Air of Savannah 93
Fernbank Museum of Natural History 12
Fernbank Science Center 14, 54
57th Fighter Group 60
Final Touch Books 14
Finster Folk Art 142
Flea Market Tubing 77
Foley House Inn 95
Folkson 67
Folkston 31
Food Studio 118
Forces of Nature 10
Forest Hills Mountain Hideaway 80
Forrest Gump 10
Forever Resorts 83
Forsyth 116
Forsythia Festival 116
Fort Discovery/National Science Center 46
Fort Valley 39
Founders Memorial Garden 42
Four Seasons 121
Fox Theatre 3, 5, 10, 22, 23
Fox Blueberry Farm 49
Foxfire Collections 34
Franklin D. Roosevelt State Park 83
Franklin 49
Fred's Famous Peanuts 48
Fried Green Tomatoes 11

Fritchey's Garden 49
Gainesville 44
Garmon's Organics 49
Gaslight Inn 135
George L. Smith State Park 29
George's 96
Georgia Department of Agriculture 47
Georgia Museum of Art 14
Georgia Covered Bridge Arts Festival 28
Georgia Shakespeare Festival 18
Georgia Renaissance Festival 17
Georgia Music Hall of Fame 8
Georgian Terrace 23
Ghost Talk, Ghost Walk 44
Glen Ella Springs Inn 82
Glen Ella Inn and Conference Center 69
Gold City Corral 66
Goldfinger 122
Golf Digest Instruction Schools 62
Good To Go 47
Greyfield Inn 106
Guido Gardens 38
Habersham Winery 120
Hammock Company 94
Hannah's East at the Pirate's House 93, 123
Happy Herman's 121
Harbor Landing 83
Harlem 11
Harrell's Vineyard 49
Haunting Tours 93
Hawkinsville 48
Hawksbell Farm 35
Hearn Academy Inn 19
Helen 48, 49, 61, 80, 84
Hiawassee 81
Hillcrest Orchards 50
Horizon Theater 16

Hot Thomas Barbeque & Peach Orchard 52
Hyatt Regency Atlanta 55
Il Centro Café 132
Imperial Fez 124
Imperial Theatre 23
Inn at Lofty Branch 82
Innsbruck Resort and Golf Club 84
Jackson Street Books 15
Jarrell Plantation 116
Jean Louise 114
Jekyll Island Club Hotel 63
Jekyll Island Museum Center 102
Jekyll Island Welcome Center 104
Jekyll Island 63, 101
Jekyll Island Club 102
Johnny Mercer Museum 8
Jordan's Bicycle Center 32
Joseph & Friends Salon and Day Spa 133
Juliette 11
Karl Bissinger's French Confections 132
Kennesaw 141
Key Lime Pie Salon and Wellness Spa 134
Knights of Columbus (Post 660) 125
Kolomoki Mounds State Historic Park 29
Lake Lanier Island Rentals 83
Lake Lanier Islands 63, 84
Last Resort Grill 14
Lawrence of Arabia 9
Lefont Plaza Theater 124
Len Foote Hike Inn 79
Lithonia 54
Lodge on Little St. Simmons Island 100
Lofty Branch 82
Loganville 42
Lookout Mountain 39

Love Potion #9 10
Juliette Gordon Low Birthplace and Museum 92
Lumpkin 28, 68, 117
Lunch Box Museum 142
Macon 8
Macon-Bibb County Convention & Visitors Bureau 53
Madison 21
Madison-Morgan Cultural Center 21
Madras 51
Majestic Food Shop 124
Marietta 114, 141
Mark of the Potter 82
Martini Club 122
Masquerade 126
Massee Lane Gardens 39
McCaysville 65
Melon Bluff 40
Metter 29, 38
Michelle's 28
Mick's 10
Midnight in the Garden of Good and Evil Book Tour 93
Midnight Star Pottery 140
Midway 41
Minnehaha Falls 75
Mistletoe State Park 47
Monastery of the Holy Spirit 141
Morris Museum of Art 12, 46
Morrow 6
Morton Theater 4
Mossy Creek Barnyard Arts & Crafts Festival 20
Mount Berry 39, 51
Mountain Memories Inn 81
Mountain City 34
Mr. John B's Restaurant 66
Mrs. Wilke's Boarding House 93

Natural Body Day Spa 134
Newnan 49, 53
North Beach Grill 95
Oak Hill Plantation 39, 51
Ocean Motion Surf Company 101
Oglethorpe University 18
Okefenokee National Wildlife Refuge 31
Old Savannah Tours 93
Old Pink House 93
Old Car City USA 143
Oliver Hardy Festival 11
Open Gates Bed and Breakfast Inn 105
Opera Athens 4
Ossabaw Island Foundation 96
Outdoor Systems Advertising 144
OutWrite 15
Panorama Orchards 50
Payne's Farm 49
Picture This 102
Pine Mountain Antique Mall 37
Pine Mountain 37, 38, 65, 66, 83
Pink Cottage 106
Polaris Lounge 55
Powers' Crossroads Country Fair and Arts Festival 53
Prater's Mill Country Fair 50
Providence Canyon Conservation Park 68
R.R. Theater 10
Red Top Mountain State Park 68
Regina's 15
Renaissance Pine Isle Resort 63
Renaissance Pine Isle Resort 84
Righteous Room 124

Rising Fawn 36
Ritz Carlton Buckhead 132
River Street Riverboat Company 115
Riverwalk Special Events 8
Robert L. Stanton Rose Garden 41
Rock City Gardens 39
Rolling Pin Kitchen Emporium 119
Rome Symphony Orchestra 7
Rome 7, 139
Roswell 86, 116, 133
Ruggiere: A Gallery 136
Rutledge 117
Sambuca Jazz Café 126
San Gennaro Italian Ristorante 4
Sapelo Island National Estuarine Research Reserve 98
Savannah 13, 14, 15, 19, 20, 42, 92, 94, 95, 109, 114, 115, 123, 140
Savannah College of Art and Design 20
Savannah Convention and Visitor's Bureau 92
Savannah Riverfront Association 92
Savannah Riverboat Cruises 44
Savannah Shadows Ghost Tour 93
Savannah Spectres and Other Strange Tales 44
Sconyer's Bar-B-Que 47
Sea Island 62, 63
Sea Island Golf Club 62
Sea Camp Ranger Station 105
Senoia 135
Seven Stages Theater 16
17Hundred90 Inn Restaurant and Lounge 115

Shellmont Bed & Breakfast 135
Ships of the Sea Maritime Museum 13
Silent Film Society of Atlanta 10
Six Flags Over Georgia 45
Skate Escape 70
Sky Valley Resort 70
Smoak's Bakery 121
Snellville 61
Social Circle 118
Southeastern Expeditions 69
Southern Images Gallery 93
Spa at Château Élan 132
Spa at Peachtree Athletic Center 133
Spa Sydell 134
Spartina Trails 94
Spivey Hall 6
Springer Opera House 23
St. Simons Island 62
St. Simons Lighthouse and Museum of Coastal History 102
St. Simons Transit Company 101, 104
Starlite Six Drive-in Theater 12
State Botanical Gardens of Georgia 42
Stephan's 144
Stone Mountain 30, 52
Stone Mountain State Park 30, 52
Stone Mountain Village 30
Stovall Mill Bridge 30
Sun Dial Restaurant, Bar, and View 55
Sweet Sunshine Equestrian Center 66
Swingers 126
Telfair Museum of Art 93
The Horse Whisperer 9
The Night the Lights Went

Out in Georgia 10
Theatre in the Square 114
Thomaston 69
Thomson 17
Thomson-McDuffie
    Tourism Bureau 17
Ticketmaster 6
Tiffany & Company 132
Tifton 18
Times on Bay 92
Tom Turpin Ragtime
    Society 20
Town & Gown Players 16
Tree Climbers International
    142
Twin City 29
Tybee Island Lighthouse
    and Museum 95
U.S. Fish and Wildlife
    Service 67
Unicoi State Park 80
University of Georgia 13
Valdosta 46
Veranda 135
Victoria's Carriages 102
Vines Botanical Gardens 42
Washington 116
Water Sports 101
Watkinsville 52, 136
Watson Mill Bridge 31
Weekender 98
Westville Village 29
When Harry Met Sally 9
Whistle Stop Café 116
White Hall Inn 81
White Water 45
Whitesburg 49
Wild Adventures 46
Wild Animal Safari 38
Wine World 121
Wired & Fired: A Pottery
    Playhouse 140
Woody's Mountain Bikes 49
Wordsworth Books 15
Wormsloe Historic Site 20,
    42

Yesterday Café 117
Zoo Atlanta 46